P9-BYJ-317

"*Power Base Selling* is a super how-to-do-it manual for salespeople who have moved up the ladder from using skills and product knowledge to business selling and new political selling. You will find the how-to manual of use not only to sales strategists but also to product managers. Finally, it's in print: it's okay to be an Ivy League street fighter and beat the competition. A must reading for all sales professionals."

Ted N. Higginson
Vice-President, Marketing Operations & Development
AT&T Network Systems

"I heartily endorse this book. It is the best book on sales proficiency that I've read. Jim Holden's book will set new standards for salesmanship—the company able to train their sales organization to this level of proficiency will definitely be a major force in a given marketplace."

Harold S. Fischer
President, Commercial Systems Division
UNISYS

"Once is not enough. If you are a professional salesperson or want to become one, then I would recommend reading this book once a year for the rest of your career."

J. Earl MacLean, Manager
Marketing Education
Data General Corporation

"Since MSA implemented Jim Holden's *Power Base Selling* methods, market share has increased, sales turnover has been cut in half, price discounting has been reduced by a third, and new people are becoming politically astute and more effective sooner. *Power Base Selling* is the way I think and sell."

John P. Imlay
Chairman and CEO
Management Science America, Inc.

"I've used Jim Holden's *Power Base Selling* techniques with three different sales organizations and in each case they became a unique and vital tool, instrumental to our eventual success. This book is creative, cogent, and an easily digested presentation of these principles."

Charles A. Winick
President, CFI Resources Inc.

"This book is a must—not to be simply read but culturalized and implemented. Holden has gone far beyond Sales 101. This work will prepare both sales and upper management for twenty-first century survival and victory. Ivy League street fighting is not for everyone. It will be useful for those intelligent and bold enough to look themselves in the mirror, 'check for bleeding,' and then make the commitment to condition themselves for a new world of intensely competitive selling."

Tracey T. Powell
President, TELCORP Inc.

"Holden first challenges and then gently prods the salesperson to *take responsibility* for the total sales process and results. Then in an entertaining style, explains how to achieve the upper levels of performance and professionalism. This is the only sales 'how-to' book that doesn't preach, condescend, or pretend that professional selling is easy."

Patrick S. Howard
President, VMX, Inc.

"Holden's book is very well written and aimed at the salespeople who are serious about being the best."

John G. Kirsch
Vice-President, Sales
Stratacom, Inc.

"A workable, practical guide to improving performance while selling into situations that require well-thought-out strategies to deal with a multiplicity of buying influences, motivations, and competitors. I recommend *Power Base Selling* as 'must' reading for anyone wishing to develop the extra margin of advantage that the superior salesperson must achieve."

James A. Prestridge
Vice-President, Component Test Group
Teradyne, Inc.

"*Power Base Selling* emphasizes the need for a more total approach to selling based on identifying and influencing the people with real power and authority. The 1990s, as Holden says, will be more about *winning* than selling—you get the feeling that it's all been a bit hit-and-miss until now."

Martin Francis
Vice-President, International Operations
LTX (Europe) Ltd.

"Jim Holden provides insight into critical components of selling often overlooked in an intensely competitive environment—highly recommended reading."

Richard A. Canada
Director, Sales & Consultant Education
Wang Laboratories, Inc.

"There are more professed experts in the area of sales and marketing than government lobbyists. A good salesman is an easy sell; a bad salesman is desperate. Therefore, instant demand for mediocre material. Holden addresses the real issues at a new level, with greater insight and with discipline. He reaches beyond anything published to date. Throw away everything else."

Steve Zelencik
Senior Vice-President and Chief Marketing Executive
Advanced Micro Devices

"Jim Holden has transcended the barriers of time, transporting the writings of Sun Tzu into the corporate boardroom of the 1990s. Jim's insights and discussions on competitive selling have defined the ground rules for success. The Power Base principle represents Holden's golden rule of competitive selling and will become the cornerstone of every sales campaign our salespeople undertake."

Rick Benoit
Manager of Sales Marketing Education
Rolm Corporation

"Jim Holden's book is a must read for those who want to build a high performance sales organization, create a competitive advantage, and out distance themselves from the competition. *Power Base Selling* is the prescription for sales organizations that want to learn how to work smarter rather than harder."

Jeff Boetticher
Chief Operating Office
Black Box Corporation

"Powerbase selling is an effective tool for both individual sales professionals and experienced sales managers. It brings focus to an often blurred vision on sales situations. Students in professional sales will benefit from this book."

Courtney S. Wang
Wang Laboratories

"Using a marker to highlight important concepts in Jim Holden's new book *Power Base Selling* is an exercise in futility. By the end of the first chapter you realize all you've done is paint each page yellow.

Jim Holden clearly recognizes that all human communication is politically motivated. Understanding what and who influences a client's decision to buy requires an investigative quality that must be internalized by today's successful sales professional. *Power Base Selling* masterfully combines the sales professional's art with that of the strategic political scientist. This book brings concepts to light that remain invisible for too many salespeople. It helps you profile any organization so that you can establish an effective networking program to obliterate your competitors. Without a doubt, those empowered with these principles will have their competition breaking out in a cold sweat."

Mike Bishop
Vice President
Union Planters Investment
Bankers Group, Inc.
Memphis, Tennessee

"I have seen the Holden Power Base Selling methodologies turn many individual accounts as well as entire companies around. It especially helps new salespeople learn to turn the normal political activity of a complex sale into competitive advantage and become victors rather than victims. This book presents the most advanced thinking in sales training today. Moreover, its successful implementation produces results."

Rick Page
President
Competitive Sales Advantage, Inc.

"The ultimate is to become so much a part of the customers' business strategy that the salesperson is viewed as an asset, an insider. This is what Jim Holden's book is all about: becoming an insider, the symbiotic relationship. It is a well-written guide to developing higher levels of sale proficiency. Jim presents valuable insights into the sales process in an interesting and highly readable style. He provides the reader with both a base philosophy and specific tools for developing and honing his/her sales career. Salespeople of all levels will enjoy this book and find dual value in it for information and inspiration."

Jim Healy
LTX/Trillium

POWER BASE SELLING

POWER BASE SELLING

Secrets of an
Ivy League
Street Fighter

JIM HOLDEN

John Wiley & Sons, Inc.
NEW YORK • CHICHESTER • BRISBANE • TORONTO • SINGAPORE

Squirt is a registered trademark of Squirtco.
PCjr. is a registered trademark of
International Business Machines Corp.

In recognition of the importance of preserving what has been
written, it is a policy of John Wiley & Sons, Inc., to have
books of enduring value published in the United States
printed on acid-free paper, and we exert our best efforts
to that end.

Copyright © 1990 by Jim Holden.
Published by John Wiley & Sons, Inc.

All rights reserved. Published simultaneously in Canada.

Reproduction or translation of any part of this work
beyond that permitted by Section 107 or 108 of the
1976 United States Copyright Act without the permission
of the copyright owner is unlawful. Requests for
permission or further information should be addressed to
the Permissions Department, John Wiley & Sons, Inc.

This publication is designed to provide accurate and
authoritative information in regard to the subject
matter covered. It is sold with the understanding that
the publisher is not engaged in rendering legal, accounting,
or other professional services. If legal advice or other
expert assistance is required, the services of a competent
professional person should be sought. *From a Declaration
of Principles jointly adopted by a Committee of the
American Bar Association and a Committee of Publishers.*

Library of Congress Cataloging-in-Publication Data

Holden, Jim, 1948–
    Power base selling / Jim Holden.
        p.   cm.
    Includes bibliographical references.
    ISBN 0-471-51033-5 (cloth) 0-471-58297-2 (paper)
    1. Sales personnel.   2. Selling.   3. Competition.   I. Title.
    HF5439.5.H65   1990
    658.8'5—dc20   89-24882

Printed in the United States of America

10 9 8 7 6 5 4 3 2

This book and the Holden Corporation are a reality because of the dedication and hard work of everyone in our company. It all began ten years ago when I started the business with little capital and even less business acumen.

What I did have, however, was a vision, and a person who trusted and supported me in abiding fashion. This book is dedicated to her: to Chris, my wife, business partner, and friend.

FOREWORD

The re-engineering of corporate America has begun. Executives in every major industry have barely been able to catch their breath after two decades of technological breakthroughs that changed the nature of management, that forced a shift in focus from production quotas and factory capacity to information and information processing. And now these same executives are confronted with a new set of business influences. We are in the midst of another industrial revolution, the transition into a service economy, and corporate life will never be the same. We are told that the corporation of the future will be down-sized, have a flatter management structure, and be forced to compete on a global scale.

The watchword today is "competitiveness"—in every aspect of a company's operations, including its sales force. No longer is a marketing organization simply a delivery mechanism, a way to get products in front of customers. More and more, the manner in which salespeople approach their task is every bit as important as the products they sell. At this critical time, along comes Jim Holden's important book, *Power Base Selling: Secrets of an Ivy League Street Fighter*. With it, the re-engineering of the sales force is now defined, and the term "added value" takes on an entirely new meaning.

Foreword

There was a time when being an account executive was tantamount to being a product representative. Then, the marketer's role expanded, and salespeople were required to develop broader business expertise and "sell solutions." But in the re-engineered organization, salespeople are required to do more: to become product, business, and *political* account executives. Customers look for vendors who can be business partners, who are willing to share risk, and who are able to manage it.

None of this makes the job of selling any easier, and as the competitive climate continues to intensify, salespeople will encounter issues that can be extremely difficult to deal with: decreased product differentiation, worldwide competition with no permanently safe markets, longer sales cycles, and shorter product-life spans. Every sales organization that intends to survive in the re-engineered corporate environment must respond to these realities. In this book, Jim Holden has put together a road map for doing so, and has given us strategies for becoming masters of the product, business, and political challenges that exist today in the profession of selling.

TED N. HIGGINSON
Marketing Vice-President
AT&T Network Systems

ACKNOWLEDGMENTS

When my sales career began in 1974, I had the great privilege of working for both an outstanding sales manager and company. Teradyne and, specifically, Jim Prestridge, then vice-president of sales, gave me a chance—even though there was a company hiring freeze at the time. Jim provided me with direction and support and taught me the principles upon which his direction was based. My sales philosophy evolved from his teachings. I will always be grateful.

Jim Healy, who was one of my first customers ten years ago and is a long-time friend and advisor, has also played a key role in my success. As you read the chapters on strategy, you will see concepts in which Jim Healy was instrumental in pioneering. He is, himself, a master strategist.

Power Base Selling, as a book, was derived from the Holden Corporation's Power Base Selling seminar, the first program in the marketplace to address competition and customer politics in a manner consistent with today's quality initiatives. I would like to thank all of our instructors who have done such an excellent job in teaching the course and inspiring salespeople with the Power Base methodology.

No acknowledgment for this book could be complete without mentioning the work of LaVon Koerner, a senior member of the Holden Corporation staff. He has made numerous enhancements to the seminar, particularly in the area of assessment, where the competitive strength of salespeople and the impact of Power Base can be measured. LaVon, or "LV" as I call him, is an inspiration to all of us.

Last, but not least, I would like to recognize our customers, who have always been at the center of our innovation. Their support and commitment to the implementation of Power Base within their sales organizations has made the Holden Corporation's mission of *"breaking glass"* a reality.

JIM HOLDEN

CONTENTS

Contents

Contents

Chapter 9
Setting a Competitive Sales Strategy
*The opportunity of defeating the enemy is
provided by the enemy himself*

Chapter 10
Street Fighting Tactics for Keeping Competitors at Bay
*The highest form of generalship is to balk
the enemy's plans*

Chapter 11
The Political Strategy
Make your way by unexpected routes

PART THREE
Zeroing In

Chapter 12
Should I Compete? Targeting Your Opportunities
*He will win who knows when to fight,
and when not to fight*

Chapter 13
Can I Win?
*He who is destined to defeat first fights
and afterwards looks for victory*

Introduction

Why Selling Skills and Good Products Are Not Enough

If you know the enemy and know yourself,
your victory will not stand in doubt.

—**Sun Tzu**

Know this about yourself: there is only one reason professional salespeople lose orders.

Suppose you are competing in a situation where your product doesn't quite measure up. You know it's a long shot, but the potential order is fairly large. Besides, your territory has been slow lately, so you begin to spend more and more time on the account. You try to minimize your product's weaknesses; you emphasize the strength of your company's reputation; you promise service and support equal to none. Still, there is a fundamental problem: the competition can deliver today, and your product's enhancements are several months down the line.

In the end, you lose the sale. Why? Because your product just can't do the job, right? The customer wants a solution now, your competition has it and you don't, so you lose. But

1

that isn't why you lose. There is only one reason professional salespeople lose orders.

Suppose you've been leading the pack in a sales campaign for a period of weeks or even months. You're sailing along, your product is clearly superior. You've developed a good relationship with the customer, who makes it clear that things look very good for you indeed. Proud and confident, you forecast the business, congratulate yourself on a job well done, and think about how to spend your commission check. But then, just when everything is going so well, the competition pulls the rug out from under you. They slash their price 40 percent, presenting to the customer an irresistible financial incentive to reevaluate the vendor selection. You alert your managers, warning them that you can't win unless they authorize a large discount. But management is unwilling to forego profit margins, and the order goes to the other vendor. You lose it, for only one reason, and not because of the competition's predatory pricing. There is only one reason salespeople lose orders:

They are OUTSOLD.

How could you be outsold when you never had a chance to win? How could you be outsold when the competition bought the business? Often, the more revealing question is not *how* you were outsold, but *when*.

If the odds were so heavily stacked against you, you may have been outsold from the very beginning. You may have lured yourself into devoting a lot of time and effort to a deal you had no business competing for. If you had known how little chance you had of winning it, would you still have fought? If so, would you have conducted your sales campaign the same way?

2

If another vendor knocked you off your feet at the very close of the sales cycle, you may have underestimated them. You may have been outsold in the critical, middle stages of the campaign, happily pitching features and benefits to every friendly ear, cheerfully ignorant of what the competition had in store for you. If you had anticipated that the decision might become price-driven, would you have taken steps to secure your position? Would you have worked harder with more people in the account to drive up the value of working with you, so the competition's fire-sale prices wouldn't have such a drastic effect?

A mature approach to the profession of selling begins with understanding that there is only that one, fundamental, reason salespeople lose orders. People who don't understand this reason are the kind who enter an account where their product, service, or price somehow puts them at a disadvantage, and resign themselves to a loss. Their sales activity becomes little more than a matter of going through the motions; defeat becomes a self-fulfilling prophecy. Even worse, they prematurely walk away from opportunities, surrendering potential business that might have developed favorably if their thinking hadn't prevented them from finding some creative way to improve their chances.

All of this implies a personal responsibility to be competitive, and that's exactly what this book is about. It will induce a fundamental shift in how you view the profession of selling.

Selling is not simply a matter of employing good sales skills to convince a customer to buy a good product. It's more like a street fight. Competitors want the same piece of business you do, so to win, you'll have to take it away from them. While it's true that you must convince the customer to buy your product, you must also take steps to prevent the competition from convincing the customer to buy theirs. You have to win the business on the streets, and you must do so with a certain Ivy League sense of class and style.

Selling Skills Are Not Enough

There are certain skills you must master to reach anywhere near your potential as a sales professional. For one, you need the *mind* of a detective to probe for your client's needs, to spot subtle buying signals, to know when to foster an open dialogue and when to ask questions that result in a simple "yes" or "no." You need the *discipline* of an architect to prepare, organize, and structure a sales call in such a way that you continuously emphasize and confirm the benefits of the creative solution you've devised. You need the *patience* and *tact* of a diplomat to establish rapport, overcome objections, clear up misunderstandings, and deal with problems or disputes.

All of these are important selling skills and most of us learn their fundamentals in training, and work to increase our proficiency at them throughout our careers. But it is important to know that traditional selling skills are not the *competitive* selling skills that are needed. Conventional techniques help you in only one dimension of the selling effort—the relationship between a seller and a buyer. To focus only on a prospective buyer implies that there is only one thing between you and getting the order—the customer. It makes the customer the major threat in the sales campaign. It produces a distorted vision of what selling is all about, and a blind spot to the real threat—the competition.

As much as you want the customer's business, so does someone else. But a typical sales campaign makes no provision for the competitive threat. The "quote and hope" mentality reigns supreme. You can bet that a competitor of yours has a few surprises up his or her sleeve in a deal you're working on right now. Imagine how different your job will be when your sales plan includes a few surprises of your own, when everything you do in the sales campaign is designed to strengthen your position with the customer *and weaken the competition* at the same time.

A complete sales approach incorporates a view of the world as it really is: a three-dimensional interplay between you, your customer, and the competition. The basics of selling get you into the game. Being competitive, and winning, requires more.

Good Products Are Not Enough

Without question, a clearly superior product produces advantage for you. In those rare, happy times when you have an exceptional product and are the only game in town, you can coast along for quite some time only on the capabilities and reputation of the product you represent. Of course, these glad circumstances mislead many people into believing they are selling well, when, in reality, the product is doing all the work with the salesperson just along for the ride. This is far more serious than a mere case of mistaken identity. If you judge yourself and your efforts by the strength of your product, you might also judge the potency of your competitors only by the strength of their products, and make a fatal error in the process. Anyone who has been selling for a while knows that the best product doesn't always win. As much as product superiority can produce competitive advantage, it can also lull you into a false sense of security.

A lot of salespeople don't sell, they surf. Their prospecting is more like searching for the perfect wave than working to make things happen in accounts. They don't create demand, they only become adept at servicing demand, identifying niches for "hot" products that have developed a certain momentum and appeal. As with champion surfers, they make the job look easy—and it may be easy, for a while, until the currents shift.

Things change. You can probably look around your own industry and see the remains of companies that sought advantage solely from product superiority. Directly or indirectly, they challenged their competitors to catch up. When their challenge was met, the advantage these companies once held disappeared—and then, *they* disappeared. But, before sinking below the horizon, something changed in their sales organizations, too. A lot of their best salespeople, the most "competitive" salespeople, the really "good" salespeople—well, they weren't so "good" anymore.

Of course, surfers can wipe out even before the unthinkable happens. No product is good enough to ensure a sale, and if your only asset is your product's strength, you'd be well advised to start looking for a soft spot in the sand. You'll begin to make grievous errors. At some point, in some sales situation, you'll write off an opponent whose product's capabilities are limited, and that salesperson will put you in the water.

Street fighters will find ways to be viable in an account despite product deficiencies. They will work to mitigate their areas of weakness, and accentuate whatever factors work in their favor. They'll get people involved in the decision-making process who you never dreamed would have a role. They'll play down the significance of their product's shortcomings by playing up the philosophical compatibility between their company and the customer from a general business point of view.

Street fighters will work with influential people in the account to alter the buying criteria, usually late in the process, to diminish their competitors' "superiority." They might even bring in other vendors, other competitors, to "network" a solution to the customer's needs, to divide the pie, or just to muddy the waters, giving the customer enough fear, uncertainty, and doubt to delay the decision for some period of time.

All of this occurs while you paddle along in peace, blissfully unaware that a riptide has been created to carry you out to sea. Of course, when you finally realize what's happening and start working harder, all your efforts only take you farther from the shore.

Superior products do not make you personally competitive any more than lacking a strong offering means that you can't compete. Of course, unless the excuse of a slightly higher price is handy, a lot of people will blame a loss on the product. But there is only one reason professional salespeople lose orders—and you know what it is. Product is important, but it isn't everything. Don't confuse your competitiveness with what it is that you sell.

It's More Than Being Aggressive

There must be a certain amount of pride in the constitution of everyone who chooses to make a career of selling. It helps to be aggressive, to be determined to win, and many people believe they are competitive because they hate to lose. There are even sales managers who try to calibrate the aggressiveness of candidates for sales positions by placing a premium on those who have competed in sports. But there is a world of difference between the aggressiveness required to excel at sports and the competitiveness needed to succeed in selling.

All sports eventually come down to one-on-one confrontations with a known entity. In selling, you may never lay eyes on the competition. Muscle, speed, and size are of paramount importance in sports. In selling, thinking, acumen, and judgment can put even the most formidable opponent at an extreme disadvantage. Most team sports are intense physical confrontations where aggressiveness must be generated to a state near frenzy; the winning team is often the one whose players are the most passionately charged during the critical parts of the game. In selling, such an intense emotional involvement actually works against you.

When a complex sales situation peaks, where something substantial is riding on the outcome and serious challenges begin to appear, about the worst thing a salesperson can do is blindly rush ahead. In sales, when the game is on the line, your actions must not be based on an emotional attachment to the objective. They must be governed by a cool, poised, incisive analysis of the situation. Confusion must be eliminated; the impulse to do something must be dominated by the disciplined determination to do the right thing.

Being an aggressive person with a will to win may help you in your sales career. It can infuse you with the energy it takes to work in an inherently contentious environment. But the object of selling is not to do battle with the competition. The object is to win, not at all costs, but with that certain Ivy League sense of class and style, to win wherever possible *before* the battle is fought. In that context, the will to *prepare* to win becomes most critical.

About twenty-five hundred years ago, Sun Tzu wrote a treatise, *The Art of War*, which has been translated many times into several languages through the ages. Recently, it has become a popular source of quotations for people who like to draw parallels between business and warfare. I'm not sure if that correlation is appropriate, but I do know that Sun Tzu's teachings offer more than entertaining aphorisms. Imbedded in his very small book is very great wisdom. For me, the relevance is not to military conflict, but to taking command over one's environment and resources, including one's thinking process.

Competitive selling is not a matter of selling harder. It is a discipline involving the development of insight and knowing what to do with it. Competitive salespeople—Ivy League street fighters—do not ignore the customary aspects of selling; they augment them by establishing themselves as a separate and distinct source of competitive advantage because of their abilities.

The process begins (in Part One of this book) with taking a different perspective on the initial approach to a sales opportunity, getting to the inside track of an organization's political structure. It continues, in Part Two, with looking at a sales situation through a window of opportunity, accurately understanding the terrain, and basing a sales approach on one of four types of strategy that will simultaneously take the wind out of the competition's sails and lead to victory. Governing the competitive process (in Part Three) will be a mechanism for zeroing in on choosing your battles well, knowing when it makes sense to compete, and determining early in time what it will take to win.

Sun Tzu's admonition to "know yourself" may have been offered to warriors twenty-five hundred years ago, but it's advice well-given to salespeople today. It is essential to know what makes you competitive, and to have sufficient will to prepare to win every time it's worth it.

Part One: The Inside Track

Chapter 1

The Power Base: Finding the People with Influence

We are not fit to lead an army unless we are familiar with the face of the country.
—Sun Tzu

The army a salesperson leads is a force of one. In that sense, you are a general. And every good general, before launching a campaign, first develops a clear vision of the terrain, "the face of the country." It is the strength of this vision that often determines the outcome of the endeavor.

Too often, salespeople don't think like generals. Their knowledge of the field of battle is limited to the most immediate needs expressed by those most obviously involved in the buying decision; they think like the foot soldiers that many in their organizations believe them to be. You may *be* your company's foot soldier, its first line of defense and attack, but you don't have to *think* like one.

One critical perspective about an account that salespeople tend to lack is of the organization's character, its personality. Salespeople scope out a limited view of an account's formal organization but fail to place it in the context of a broader picture, and rarely gain clarity about the informal structure—the Power Base—that really makes an organization tick. Without this clarity, it's almost impossible to get a sense of the larger issues that will truly determine your ability to compete for business and win it.

If you've been selling for some time, you know the power of organizational politics. In every company, every department, and every business unit, a game is being played. For the salesperson, the trick is to know the rules of the game and the part you can legitimately play.

Many of us are warned to keep a proper distance from the political aspects of an account—to observe them, but not to get involved. But whether you know it or not, and whether you like it or not, you *are* involved. To win business, you have to sell enough people on your ideas, and you have to sell the *right* people. Every time we talk about the "right" people, people with clout, we're talking about politically powerful people, so we're dealing with politics. Only one question remains: are you going to be a passive victim, or are you going to gain competitive advantage by being politically astute?

Political Competition

One of the reasons many people disdain politics is because the word conjures up negative images. "Internal politics" implies that people are competing within an organization, *against each other*, and that *must* be bad. Well, it isn't bad at all. In fact, nothing could be more natural, and few things contribute so significantly to an organization's health. After all, every form of life needs a natural selection process for its species to grow, for the strong to rise to positions of leadership, and for the weak to be either protected or culled out. An organization also needs this same process. There simply isn't enough room at the top of a corporation for everyone who would like to be in a pivotal position, where a company needs its best people. Someone who wants to rise to the top will have to compete with others by proving that he or she is one of those "best" people. Nature demands it.

The competition for advancement is the most obvious political activity to observe, but people also compete for other, more fundamental, reasons. For one, people must vie for influence every day simply to do their jobs. For another, since no company has unlimited assets, the competition for precious resources is often the most intense.

In the annual battle of the budget, every department in a company must compete with one another to get an adequate head count. When staffing-up for a project, managers compete to get good people into their organizations. Once they have them, they must compete to keep them. As the project they're working on gets underway, a variety of interested parties will jockey for position and reach for the reins, so project leaders must constantly compete for control.

All of this political competition is very natural and because it *is* so natural, companies are formally organized to create it and capitalize on it. A separation of powers in an organization produces a system of checks and balances, and a motivating influence that tends to bring out the best in people when it's well managed.

Programmed Conflict

Suppose an engineering department proposes to increase the technical capability of an existing product with improvements

15

that, unfortunately, will necessitate a higher selling price. The marketing department looks at these enhancements from a sales point of view and concludes that a higher price will adversely affect elasticity of demand, driving the product outside an already price-sensitive market. Which department will prevail?

Usually, a series of negotiations will ensue between the two groups. Marketing might urge engineering to incorporate less costly enhancements; engineering might insist that marketing develop ways to project added value to customers, thus justifying an increased price. Somewhere between the agendas of the two departments, an agreement will be found.

Without such built-in competition, there would be chaos. Companies dominated by unchecked engineering departments often manufacture an array of dazzling products that will never find a home. And marketing-driven companies frequently suffer from fragmented product lines, countless variations of similar products meant to satisfy every possible customer need, a tendency to sell "futures," and a proclivity for heavy discounting.

In healthy organizations, these two powerful forces keep each other in balance. There may be some pitched political battles along the way, but the ongoing competition eventually produces what is best for the company *and* for its customers.

A department's responsibilities can be spelled out in a written charter, but how it must interact with other functions cannot be specified in such a formal agreement. There are also no written guidelines about politics for individual employees. People do find their own ways, however, and it is simply understood that as they strive for their goals, they will have to contend with the desires of others.

It's all part of the game, but it's a good game, as long as people act in the best interests of the organization while improving their own positions. As they do, and as they succeed, an informal political structure begins to form.

The Political Structure

For a business to be organized, it must have a formal structure—a clear distribution of authority and responsibilities. Most organizations take pains to make this distribution clear, to remove any doubt about what people are responsible for what areas of endeavor. So, an organization chart, where clean lines portray a systematic delegation of authority, responsibilities, and tasks, depicts the *official* structure.

Certainly, it's important in selling to understand the official organization chart, and to gather information about the people who are directly involved in a decision. But a look at a chart doesn't tell you much about the character of the organization itself, so for that, you need to view the informal hierarchy, the *political* structure.

Unlike the official organization, the political structure is usually unclear, rarely visible to the naked eye, and never published for public consumption. The political structure of an organization is its Power Base, and the people in the Power Base are those who have political strength, who have *influence*.

The first mistake many salespeople make as they try to get "inside" an account is to confuse this influence with *authority* when, in fact, the two are not necessarily synonymous. Authority is found in the formal structure, influence in the informal one. The reason salespeople may confuse the two is because it is certainly possible, even common, for people to exert influence based on their authority. They take what power is formally allocated to them and use it to shape the organization, to make decisions, and to set direction. However, it is also possible

17

for some people to exert influence when they don't have authority. They do this by virtue of their *association* with authority—when they can act "in the name" of someone who has official responsibility.

In selling, we've all come across people who are influential in the buying process, but who have no authority. These people may be secretaries or assistants who can either provide or deny you access to a key decision maker. They may be somewhat junior-level employees, perhaps in an entirely unrelated department, whose views become central to the buying criteria because their experience is valued by the right people. They may be consultants, with no authority at all, who, by their association with the managers who hired them, are able to tap into influence and increase their own power.

It is therefore a mistake to assume that those with authority automatically influence a decision, and a serious error to believe that people who lack authority have no influence in a sales situation. Figure 1.1 shows how those who have authority may or may not have influence, and how people may have influence despite a lack of authority.

Authority and Influence

Those in the upper-left-hand corner of Figure 1.1, "Influential Authoritarians," have both authority and influence. They have official responsibility. They are at or near the top of the organization chart, whether it is that of a company, a division, or a department. They also have political influence because they are known to use their legal power to steer the organization, to set its priorities, and to establish formal and informal expectations.

On the national scene, one could say that the president of the United States is almost always an Influential Authoritarian:

Influential Authoritarians	Non-Influential Authoritarians
Influential Non-Authoritarians	Non-Influential Non-Authoritarians

Figure 1.1. Influence vs. authority matrix.

there is no one higher on the federal organization chart. The president has the authority to direct the entire government, including the armed services. Using his authority, he can set the agenda for his administration. By exercising the influence that is *associated* with his authority, he can affect the condition and essential nature of the country, and the world.

In looking at an organization chart, one knows that the top person in a company or department has authority. One cannot, however, necessarily assume that this individual has influence.

Authority without Influence

The quadrant in the upper-right-hand corner of Figure 1.1 is for the "Non-Influential Authoritarians," those people who, despite their ex officio power, do not exert influence in matters of substance for the organization. For one reason or another, these are figureheads who hold their position for some purpose, but who don't have a role in the overall actions and passions of the organization.

On the national scene, the vice-president of the United States is frequently a Non-Influential Authoritarian. He is high on the organization chart (there's nothing wrong with being number two), but in the overall scheme, usually plays only a supporting role. Other than the constitutionally defined function of presiding over the Senate, the vice-president can act to shape the philosophy of the government only to the extent the president allows him. However, such opportunity is rarely provided, and is always performed within severely restricted limits.

In companies, Non-Influential Authoritarians may be "empty suits" who are allowed to bide their time until retirement, while the enterprise grows around them. Or, they may be people who are valued as administrators, but who are not perceived as visionaries who can lead the organization into the future. They may be viewed as people who excel at carrying out policy, but who have little to contribute to the creation of policy itself. Salespeople, wanting to connect themselves with powerful people, would spin their wheels for a long time if they relied on Non-Influential Authoritarians.

No Authority, No Influence

It would be a boon for you always to be able to align yourself with Influential Authoritarians. Unfortunately, these people are the most difficult to gain access to. So, for the majority of salespeople, the only alternative is to deal with lower-level people in the account. Working at the lower levels does have advantages. Typically, these employees are more accessible and more tuned in to the details of the need or application that is being addressed. Unfortunately, that command of detail may not necessarily do you any good.

The quadrant in the lower-right-hand corner of Figure 1.1 is reserved for the Non-Influential Non-Authoritarians (NINAs). These are some of the people you'll find at low levels on the organization chart. They have no authority, and haven't yet established enough credibility to induce those in power to seek out their views and give them an informal role in important matters. Of course this does not mean they are unintelligent or unworthy in any way. Many times, they are extremely bright, dedicated, and talented professionals. They are, however, followers. An organization relies on them to carry out certain functions, but restrains them from taking any significant initiative. To get anything done in an account, either before or after a sale, you have to work with these people quite a bit, perhaps the majority of the time. They are important, but *they don't drive sales*. They service their company's needs, and when you work with them, you only service demand.

Servicing demand is different from creating demand, or creating sales opportunities. Demand creation is the highest order of competitive selling. It enables you to work where you want to work, and to set the pace for the competition. But you just can't do it when working only at lower levels.

It's a trap salespeople fall into where they can end up spending all their time with Non-Influential Non-Authoritarians. They rely on them alone for direction and guidance, which they can't dependably provide. After all, they have a restricted role, and, at times, don't know their own limitations. Most professional salespeople have heard a familiar refrain at least once in their careers, as expressed by a "decision maker": "I'm responsible for the evaluation, and I'll be making the decision. You won't need to deal with anyone else. And, frankly, I'd prefer that you not approach my management, since they've assigned *me* this task."

Is this person trying to boost his ego at your expense? Sometimes, yes. But other times, his manager *wants* him to feel completely responsible for the project because if he does, the company will get a strong commitment in return from him, and thus can be confident that certain tasks will be definitely carried out. Nevertheless, the manager's confidence only goes so far. In the eleventh hour, as an evaluation peaks, management may well influence the decision, steering it in the direction they think is best.

So, when you hear those words from a lower-level person, one who clearly lacks authority and has no known record of being influential, and who may have blocked you from other people in the account, I suggest you do the following: check yourself for wounds, because, I assure you, you are bleeding. Somewhere in the organization, some competitor is dealing with an influential person who knows what the *real* buying criteria are, a person who can shape the criteria to favor a particular vendor if he or she sees value in doing so. The revised specifications will eventually be passed down to your contact, and you'll learn about them at some point—when it's too late, when the order is about to be placed with the competition.

Influence without Authority

The good news is, not all people who lack authority also lack influence. In the lower-left-hand corner of Figure 1.1 are Influential Non-Authoritarians. These are people who have established themselves as credible resources to those in authority for assisting in setting direction, establishing policy, and forming standards and expectations.

Back at the national scene, for many presidents the First Lady is a key resource and a trusted adviser, even though she has no authority and does not appear on the government's organization chart in any capacity. But Nancy Reagan wasn't the first, and won't be the last, presidential spouse to have a major say in who becomes a player in the administration and who gets relegated to the bench. By her association with authority, any First Lady is most certainly an Influential Non-Authoritarian in the affairs of state.

In the affairs of business, those who are driving organizations must create a support system for themselves. *They must delegate*—it is a matter of survival. By delegating, they extend their capacity. They become able to indirectly accomplish things that time constraints prevent them from achieving directly.

Some matters that are delegated are ordinary and routine and can be delegated to just about anyone. But other matters are so critical they must be delegated to those employees who are most trustworthy. Non-authoritarians become influential when, at some point, they demonstrate that they can be trusted to carry out such important duties and produce the kind of results desired by those in higher official positions. Moreover, in the course of accomplishing tasks, they provide real value when they perform in a *manner* that is valued by management. As a result, as time goes on, they are assigned to other high-value responsibilities, and their input is sought on key issues. And this is why people compete for "plum" projects—because to be successful in them builds for the future. With success, people can become part of the support structure, the Power Base, of the organization's most powerful individuals.

Determining who has authority is easy: one glance at the organization chart tells all. Determining who has influence is more involved. In sales, knowing which people are influential is knowing which people must be sold. The competitive sales campaign involves many individuals, but focuses on the few who have the power to make things happen.

Identifying Influence

Early in their careers, salespeople are taught that they will get the best results when they establish rapport with people in an account. There are a number of very valuable training programs that help salespeople draw upon their personal abilities and hone a well-defined set of "people skills." These techniques are used to search for common areas of interest with our customers, to establish a strong personal relationship. In the course of getting to know people, we naturally engage in friendly, casual discussions.

Frankly, these discussions can do a great deal more than merely demonstrate to a customer that you are personable. And the information you gather from them can be much more significant than finding out who the customer thinks will win the World Series this year. They also offer an opportunity to learn where the customer stands in the Power Base of the organization.

Identifying influence is a prerequisite to being able to tap internal power and increase your competitive strength in an account. Salespeople build rapport to enhance relationships. *Competitive* salespeople build rapport to enhance relationships *with the right people*. This allows them to become, essentially, a part of the Power Base in their own right. They'll never have authority, but they can build influence. Chapter 3 discusses in much more detail some of the characteristics of influential people, especially those who are *most* influential, the Foxes. For now, there are four common signs of the exertion of influence.

1. *Where the Action Is.*   Unlike authority, influence is usually invisible. It can only be seen when it is being

used, so it is typically visible only in times of change. To spot influence, then, a salesperson must be observant in an account's organization when things are changing, or must be able to reconstruct what transpired when things were changing in the past. Influential people in an organization can always be found having some role in major projects or activities that a company or a department is undertaking.

2. *Subtle Acknowledgments of Respect.* Organizations frequently form committees or task forces, which cross formal lines of authority, to devise an approach to a problem or some specific need. There may be seven people on the committee, but you'll often find that only one of them is the most powerful. If you were observing the committee in action, you probably wouldn't see an overt display of power, but you might witness a subtle acknowledgment of someone's clout. For example, during the course of a meeting, you might notice that one person, who has been silent most of the time, makes a simple comment—and changes the whole direction of the meeting. The exertion of influence thus becomes visible.

3. *Access.* Influential people always seem to be involved in key decisions that are made in the organization. Although there is a formal chain of command, some people have the right to bypass it to express their point of view or to steer the decision in a certain direction. Their influence becomes visible. Sometimes, upper management itself bypasses the chain of command to reach down into the organization to seek out these people. Again, influence becomes visible.

25

4. *Acting in Exception to Policy.* Let's say you're working
    in an account that, for the time being, has imposed a
    formal freeze on hiring. You may find, however, one
    manager who can still work the system to make an
    authorized position appear, to get it funded, and maybe
    even to get his or her candidate compensated at a
    higher rate than the established ceiling for the position.
    You've just found a member of the Power Base, because
    the ability to work in exception to policy is a solid
    indicator that a person has influence.

Gauging Influence

Salespeople can assess the level of influence of an individual
while engaged in one of those casual conversations. You'll find
that people have two favorite topics, neither of which is your
company or your product. People generally like to talk about
themselves, and what they do.

Instead of being a rather aimless chat, a casual conversation can be an opportunity for customers to share with you
what interests them most, and an opportunity for you to learn
about their influence. It's generally not the kind of talk you
have in a formal setting, across a conference table. It's more
impromptu, such as walking down the hall, on the way to get
a cup of coffee.

Where does this person see the department going? How
do things seem to work in the organization? What will be
some of the key challenges in meeting goals? What are the
financial issues involved in meeting them? Which people will
be counted on to get the job done? Who, at a higher level,
is providing direction and support? Who seems to have the
ear of upper management? What is the nature of that rela-

tionship? Who hired the person? Answers to all of these questions, and the dialogue that ensues from their being asked, will give you information that has strategic significance. You will also get credit for showing a genuine interest in the customer's organization. Of course, if your interest isn't genuine, you will quickly be perceived as someone who is going through the motions. But, as you read through the rest of this book, you'll discover all the practical reasons for having such a genuine interest.

Drawing the Power Base

Figure 1.2 shows a detail of an organization chart for the marketing division of a medium-sized manufacturing company. This is the official structure, the distribution of authority.

From this chart, we know that marketing is headed by a vice-president who has three directors reporting to him: one each in the Western, Central, and Eastern United States regions. Each of these directors has a sales unit manager and a technical support manager reporting to him.

For many salespeople, this chart, with a biography of each of the players, plus some knowledge of perceived product needs, would represent the sum total of their insight to the account. But we've established that there is much more to be known. Behind this official structure is a political one, a Power Base of the influential individuals in the organization. Suppose that, over the course of talking to some of these people or to others close to them, we've gained some political insight. We know that the vice-president is new to his position and perceives that he has inherited a problem in the Western regional director. We also learn that the vice-president helped the Eastern regional director get his job, even before the vice-president

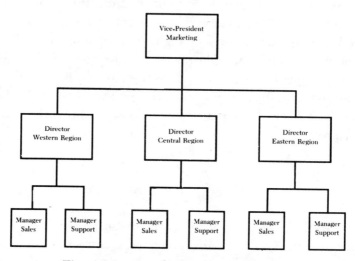

Figure 1.2. Sample organization chart.

joined the company. By our discussion with others, you learn he relies heavily on the Central regional director for advice on how a new product should be marketed, in terms of sales goals and compensation incentives.

All of this has been learned in one or two passing conversations with the right people, so we can now draw some conclusions about the Power Base at the upper level of this organization, such as assuming that the Central and Eastern regional directors are influential. We can safely say that the Western director is not.

Over time, we discover even more about this organization. Because of lack of confidence in the Western regional director, the vice-president of marketing relies heavily on the Western sales unit manager, preferring to deal with the manager directly, whenever possible, and has communicated an open-door policy, should the manager have an issue to discuss directly with the vice-president. Also, we discover that the sales unit manager in the Central region is viewed as a good administrator, but as somewhat unimaginative. On the other hand, the technical support manager there has demonstrated a flair for marketing, and has even been asked by the vice-president to comment on how support programs throughout the country can be improved.

With this additional insight, we now have an even clearer vision of the Power Base of this organization. The sales manager in the Western region and the support manager in the Central region have developed an association with authority outside their formal scopes. They are, in their particular ways, exerting influence. They have not been given any formal charter for their extra roles; they are Influential *Non*-Authoritarians. But, because they have influence, they, too, belong in the Power Base.

Figure 1.3 shows how the Power Base, the influential body, can be overlaid on the formal organization chart. In doing so, we've made visible what is usually invisible. While the organization chart depicts the distribution of authority, we can now see the distribution of influence.

A salesperson working on this account would obviously be making a huge error by taking direction from the Western regional director, no matter how strong their relationship may be. Even if this director happened to be the formal decision maker on some matter, the real decision would be made elsewhere.

Let your competition make this kind of error. Let them backtrack and change their approach several times because they get a different story from everyone they talk to. Make them sweat when they see you've signed in for a meeting with

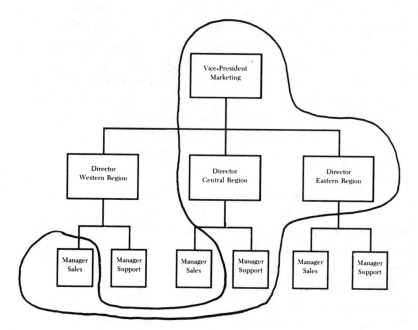

Figure 1.3. The Power Base.

someone they can't get an appointment with. Your connection to influential people can put you on the inside track, where the ride is a lot more smooth.

Your ability to do this initially will be determined by your understanding of the organization's personality, its political character. In addition, there's a fundamental principle that people who want to become influential must live by: the Power Base Principle. In Chapter 2 you'll find out how it works in organizations, and begin identifying how it can work for *you*.

Chapter 2

The Power Base Principle: How Value to the Company and Recognition Build Power

Walk in the path defined by rule.

—Sun Tzu

There is a great American myth that if you work hard and do a good job, you will get ahead. This is a fantasy. People who subscribe to it are the same ones who put copious hours and dedication into their work, all in the belief that their careers will be justly enhanced.

A successful career doesn't happen by accident or by hard work alone. People who become influential in their organizations find the path that leads into the Power Base not by stumbling upon it, but by learning the rules of the game—sometimes the hard way—and learning the Power Base Principle. So salespeople who want to gain competitive advantage by connecting with these people must acquire the same knowledge.

Let's take a look inside an organization that is about to make a major buying decision connected with an important

project. John Andrews, an ambitious, young, first-level manager, has been given responsibility to evaluate and select a
vendor. Although final approval rests with John's boss, George
McCullough, and the division's vice-president, Fred Pearson,
the decision is primarily John's. We don't need to go into the
details of this company's business, or the kind of project they're
undertaking, or even the specifics of the product or service
they're looking to acquire. Simply put your product, and maybe
even one of your customers, into the picture as we go along.

Andrews goes about his task. He creates a set of broad
categories for features he believes the product will need to
have. He develops a list of vendors who may offer those capabilities, and issues a Request for Proposal (RFP).

The sales process commences. Imagine that you are one
of the vendors who respond to the RFP and begin making
sales calls. But let's not complicate this too much. Step ahead
a few weeks: your proposal is solid, you did a good job selling,
and you have won the order. Naturally, your job isn't finished
once you have the purchasing contract in hand—there's more
work to do. Whether you sell group health insurance, manufacturing equipment, travel services, computers, or anything
in a highly competitive environment that represents a major
investment by a customer, a plan must be created to *install*
your solution and *make it work*.

In real life, this process can be challenging and somewhat
complex, and it is no different in this example. You and your
team work hard with John and his team to overcome whatever
difficulties arise and in the end, your product goes in, and is
successful. With its implementation, tangible changes will be
seen in how this organization operates. Salespeople are usually
good at observing these direct effects, and are adept at storing
them away in memory, saving them for some point in the

future when another sales opportunity presents itself in this account.

But the most interesting organizational effects don't start when the new product is installed. They begin to appear very early—in John Andrews' case, at the moment he is assigned the project. These are *intangible* effects; their impact is indirect. They represent the political ramifications of someone trying to make something happen in an organization. Characteristically, salespeople aren't adept at observing these phenomena but they should become so because they represent a real opportunity for you to gain strength.

It so happens that the business of this company is growing so rapidly that management is pondering a major expansion. For his division, Fred Pearson is considering creating a new department, and whoever he names to run it will be on the same level as George McCullough. None of this is going to happen right away—probably a year or so down the line. As John Andrews is an ambitious young man, it's a safe bet that he would like to be in a position to head the new department when it's created. In the project he's just completed, evaluating and selecting a vendor, he's been successful and has done a good job. As a result of his good work, do you suppose that John has significantly improved his chances of getting ahead? It would be nice if the answer were "yes." It is possible that the answer is "maybe." But the most politically astute answer is "no."

You know people who have worked hard their whole lives, who have done a good job throughout their careers, and who have never gotten ahead. While *not* doing a good job can get you fired, "doing a good job" never guarantees anyone will advance in an organization. Success, on the other hand, requires something extra.

Let's say that John Andrews did more than a "good job"—he brought something else to the table. John didn't just take his marching orders from management to create the criteria for vendor selection, he worked with others to develop a more in-depth perspective of the organization's needs. He looked beyond his own department to see if he could learn from anyone who had dealt with similar issues, or if there were other needs that could be folded into whatever solution he proposed. He worked with you, the vendor, to come up with a more innovative approach to his company's requirements than what an off-the-shelf solution would offer. He looked past the short-term needs to make a decision that would also allow maximum flexibility in the future. He didn't just go out and execute policy, he saw the big picture, and linked everything he did to the larger, pressing, business issues facing his company. In a word, he provided something special in the results of his efforts and the way he went about them: *value*. For him, doing a "good job" meant focusing on supplying the greatest possible value to his organization.

Now, knowing what you do, and knowing that Andrews provided value to the organization, will he get ahead? Yes or no? The best answer still remains, at this point, "no." Just as you know hard-working people who are not moving up, you know people who provide real value, but who have reached a premature plateau in their careers.

"Value" is only *one* component of the Power Base Principle. It's a ticket that gets you into the theater, but it doesn't get you the seat you want. Why doesn't someone like John Andrews advance when he represents such significant value? What else does he need?

John can provide all the value in the world, but it doesn't mean anything if *the right people don't know about it*. The second component of the Power Base Principle is *recognition*.

Value plus recognition builds power. The value John represents must be recognized by the right people—in this case, senior management. Furthermore, the value John *believes* he represents must truly *be* of value to those right people—specifically, to Fred Pearson. All the creative things John did to provide value will amount to nothing if Fred doesn't recognize they're of value, or know that John is doing them.

Let's expand our story a bit, and say that all of this has occurred. The way Andrews goes about his task, and the results he obtains, are truly valuable in Fred Pearson's eyes. He likes what he sees in John's performance and approach. Now, is John going to get ahead? Has he substantially improved the odds of winning a promotion? The answer is "yes." Of course, when the final decision is made, other factors will have to cooperate. John must be fundamentally qualified for the job, and might have to prevail over another equally impressive candidate. But he has taken the first step on a path defined by this rule:

VALUE + RECOGNITION = POWER

Value plus recognition builds power. Value, when it is recognized, increases one's political influence. As soon as Fred Pearson recognizes that John Andrews' approach to his task and the results he obtained have contributed value, an informal bond begins to develop between the two. Andrews now has an association with authority, the same kind discussed in Chapter 1 that creates influence.

What will happen as time goes on? As the organization faces new challenges, or must take on similar projects, who do you suppose Fred Pearson will rely upon? To whom will he delegate other important matters? You guessed it—John Andrews. As this occurs, the bond between Pearson and Andrews will get stronger and more visible, and will manifest itself in a number of ways.

In the beginning, it might appear simply as a casual acknowledgment. Fred may pass by as John is having lunch with his colleagues in the cafeteria. He might stop for a moment and chat with John—something that he doesn't do with many other people. He might develop a habit of dropping by John's office from time to time just to bounce a few ideas off John, or to update him on some matter. He doesn't do this with any of John's colleagues. As the bond grows stronger, one might find John in Pearson's office on a fairly regular basis. Andrews will have informal access to Pearson, while his colleagues must go through formal channels.

None of this interaction goes unnoticed to John's colleagues, and you can imagine how a lot of them react. John's increasing influence developed from the value he provided above and beyond the call of duty, and because Pearson recognized and acknowledged that value. But, to many of John's peers, he's simply "kissing up to the boss." Within an organization, this kind of negative reaction will manifest itself somewhere between petty discomfort and an all-out inability to work with or cooperate with each other.

Of course, not all of John's co-workers will respond that way. Some will be more astute; some will have a bit of savvy. These are the people who understand that politics isn't poison, but a fact of life. These people will start to approach their work the way John does. They'll model their behavior after his, and the brightest ones may even work to hitch their wagons to his star.

No matter which way it works, regardless of whether people react positively or negatively to John's entry into the Power Base, something is happening in this organization. Friction is building, friction that will have to be dealt with.

I've deliberately left out someone from the progress of our story. Look at Figure 2.1. Remember George McCullough, John's boss? As John's influence is building, as the bond between he and Pearson grows stronger, how does George feel? Just as with John's colleagues, it could go either way. One would hope that every manager at McCullough's level would be happy with John's success, or that every "McCullough" would see his or her job as that of bringing in good people, grooming them, and helping them succeed. One would dream that every manager one ever worked for would be mature enough not to be threatened by a subordinate's achievements. Maybe George McCullough is one of those managers. But a lot of people in his position aren't. Insecurity can cause people to do strange things, and people in management positions aren't immune from insecurity.

If McCullough is weak, if he has an *inflated* ego instead of a *strong* ego, he *can't* let Andrews succeed. In his mind, something about John's success suggests that *he* is a failure.

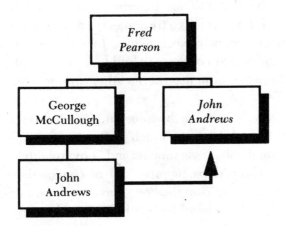

Figure 2.1. Authority matched to influence.

He will somehow see John's growing visibility as a diminution of his own, and try to put the brakes on it.

There are a number of ways weak managers can make life difficult for someone like John Andrews. They suddenly shift from a management role into a role that supervises people who ceased to need supervision long ago. They interpose themselves in every step of the process, attending every project meeting—even though they may have little to offer in the way of direct substance—and controlling the agenda. They insist that every memo and every report bear their signature. They slow things down, sometimes to the point of killing the project.

The worst of these weak managers can actually become vicious. They start keeping tabs. They spread rumors. They become clock watchers. A ruthless McCullough could hamper John's ability to do his job by imposing unreasonable administrative burdens.

Again, you would hope that McCullough wouldn't be this kind of person, but it could go either way. And, as with John's colleagues, something is happening: friction is building.

As the bond continues to grow between Andrews and Pearson, as John develops a track record, as Pearson continues to delegate high-value projects to him, John's influence, political strength, and power continue to build, at some point reaching a stage where his influence is critically disproportionate to his authority.

Some ways to correct the imbalance immediately come to mind, but they don't make much sense. For example, an organization might shift assignments and responsibilities, or even reorganize whole departments, and of course these efforts would become very complicated, particularly in larger organizations. Besides, the objective behind such reorganization is all wrong since its intent is to try to diminish John's informal strength by altering the formal structure.

Influence is potent because it is derived from value and recognition, and it is certainly strong enough to withstand half-hearted measures such as revised job descriptions. Once Pearson recognizes the value of John Andrews, he will find John, wherever he may be; he will use Andrews to help meet his business goals.

So, trying to decrease John's influence isn't the answer, but what is? Instead of lowering the river, is there a way to raise the bridge? Of course there is.

A year has passed since that first project where John started building his political power, and where organizational friction began to mount. In that time, Andrews has continued to gain recognition for the value he contributes. The company is now ready to form the new department, and the opportunity exists to redress the organizational problem created by John's increased political strength. Rather than attempting to decrease his influence, management simply increases his authority. In this story, something significant about the political dynamics of an organization should have become clear. An increase in John Andrews' authority *followed* his increased influence. That's an important fact of life to keep in mind about organizations. Many people believe that if they're given the right position, they'll finally get a chance to "do something." Just the reverse is true. One must first *do something* to get what one *wants*. What one must *do* is apply the Power Base Principle, finding ways to provide the right value and make sure the right people know it.

There's another piece of this story that I've chosen not to elaborate upon until now. Do you remember which vendor was selected? *You* were. As a result, did you somehow play a role in John's success in the long run? In the way I told the story, you did have a role, but it was a bit part. You made a cameo appearance with a good product. You won an order because you sold it well in the very traditional sense. Yes, your product worked well, and yes, its success started Andrews down his path. His initial opportunity to provide value and get recognized for it led to other opportunities and other successes. Eventually, he won a coveted position. All of these things happened. But you didn't *make* them happen.

Come to think of it, the way I told the story, John Andrews is a pretty remarkable guy. He knew how to approach his project in a way that senior management would most highly value. He knew that a new department would soon be created, and that success in his project would give him a shot at running it. But what if he wasn't so sharp? What if he didn't know what was going on in the organization? What if he didn't have a fix on Fred Pearson's values? What if he didn't realize that his buying decision represented more than simply selecting a product, but was actually his first crack at becoming a member of the Power Base?

Is there a way for you to fill this void and, as a result, gain a tremendous competitive edge? There sure is. You see, Ivy League street fighting is making the Power Base Principle work for you so that it can work for someone like John Andrews. An Ivy League effort adds indirect, political benefits for the right people to the direct, tangible benefits that must exist for the customer organization.

So far, we know some important things about the Ivy League street-fighting sales campaign. We know that behind every formal organization there is an informal political structure, the Power Base, which is the body of people who have influence regardless of their level of authority. We know that people become influential by providing value that is recognized by powerful people, and we know that a salesperson can become powerful by applying this same principle.

You can develop synergy with someone like John Andrews, but we'll come back to him a little later. For now, it's time to learn a few things about Foxes.

Chapter 3

Foxes: Finding the Heart of the Power Base

A clever fighter is one who not only wins,
but excels at winning with ease.

—Sun Tzu

A t the end of every episode, after the villains are either dead or behind bars, grateful townsfolk turn to thank their hero—and his faithful companion, Tonto—but he is gone. Who was that masked man? The job is done, and there's no time for glory when you're the Lone Ranger.

In a way, some people in organizations are a bit like that, but not because they have a penchant for being mysterious. There are practical reasons why powerful people work quietly, behind the scenes, while less skillful fighters engage in noisy, public confrontations.

I call these people Foxes. Think about it for a moment. When you imagine a fox, certain characteristics are bound to come to mind. Foxes are known to be intelligent, clever, and resourceful creatures who outthink—outfox—their opponents.

They're quiet and patient, and are never highly visible. They know the value of keeping a low profile.

At the heart of every Power Base—at the center of influence—is one person (sometimes more) who is most powerful, around whom the political structure of an organization revolves. That person is a Fox.

One ironic fact about Foxes is that the more powerful, the more truly foxlike they are, the harder they are to see. But, for the trained eye, they leave behind their own version of a single silver bullet.

A Fox in Action

Here is the story of a hypothetical corporation. Its Fox is fictional, but her characteristics are very true to life, and, incidentally, not different from those of most Ivy League street fighters. In fact, there is a natural affinity between Foxes and competitive salespeople.

Carol Miller is the vice-president of marketing at a medium-sized manufacturing company in the Midwest. Her role in the firm has grown to such an extent that she is the most influential member of the corporate Power Base—the Fox—as seen in the organization chart depicted in Figure 3.1.

Overlaid on the organization chart, the Power Base can take on a fairly strange shape. Notice something odd about this one: there is a person in the manufacturing department named Bill Thomas who is in the Power Base, but manufacturing's vice-president is not. That means Bill is more influential than his boss in the overall scheme of corporate affairs—an interesting situation. Let's see how this came to pass.

Five years ago, Carol Miller traveled to Boston to attend a class reunion at her alma mater. She reacquainted herself

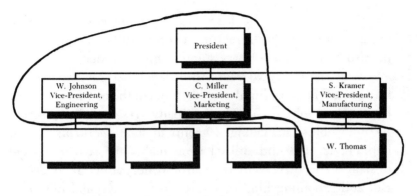

Figure 3.1. The Fox at the heart of the power base.

with a number of former classmates, and also with a few of her favorite professors. One of them invited her to lunch the next day, and asked if he could bring along someone he would like Carol to meet, a graduate student named Bill Thomas, with whom he was particularly impressed. Carol readily agreed. The next day, Carol could see why the professor was so taken by this student. Bill was bright, articulate, and had the confident air of a young man decidedly on his way up in the world. Before they finished lunch, Carol offered him a summer internship at her company, and Bill accepted.

After that summer, Bill returned to Boston to finish his studies. Shortly before graduation, he received a formal offer to join the marketing division of Carol's company. For the next year and a half, Bill established himself as a valuable resource in marketing. He won the respect of senior managers in the company, and earned a reputation in the field as being one of the rare home office people who could get things done. When a management position in marketing became vacant, Carol Miller's decision about who to promote into it was simple. Bill adapted to a management role with ease. By watching

45

Carol in action, he had learned a lot about how to keep an organization running smoothly, even in difficult times. Now he also had a chance to try some of his own ideas.

Over the next two years, Bill developed his department into one of the most highly visible units in the company. Then, he changed jobs within the company. He took the position he now holds, managing a group in *manufacturing*. What happened? How did Bill go from mahogany row to a steel desk at the factory? Why did Carol Miller, after "discovering" Bill and grooming him for five years, simply hand him over to manufacturing?

You can imagine what many people in the company thought: Bill Thomas's star had fallen. But take another look at the illustration of the Power Base. Bill is a member, he is influential. His move was hardly a defeat. In fact, it was a great victory, and his presence in manufacturing represents a boon to Carol Miller. She now has a trusted ally, a key lieutenant, in a pivotal position in another division, a division that competes with hers for funding and control.

I should tell you something else about this organization. In about six months, the vice-president of Manufacturing is going to retire. Who do you suppose is his heir apparent? You guessed it—Bill Thomas. And Bill's elevation to an executive position will be as advantageous for Carol Miller as was his move to manufacturing in the first place. As we examine the benefits for her, two imperatives for Foxes will be revealed.

The Organization Comes First

One advantage for Carol is that the organization gets Bill, one of its most talented people, into an important position. Every true Fox operates in such a manner; their actions are governed by the principle that everything they do must strengthen the organization in some way. Foxes who don't live by this maxim aren't really Foxes. They may have a lot of the same characteristics, they may be every bit as intelligent, strategically oriented, and resourceful as the Foxes I've described so far. But if they don't put the organization first, if they act only on the basis of what will benefit *them* the most, without regard to the good of the company, they aren't like foxes at all. They're more like weasels.

For me, an ideal Fox is the character Obi Wan Kenobi in George Lucas's *Star Wars*. The truest Foxes, the ones who are going to endure, have "the force" behind them, *the power of principles, ethics, and positive intent*. Find people like that in your accounts, and find a way to offer them the most value you possibly can. You will learn, and you will prosper. Just beware of the Darth Vaders; there is a dark side of the force. Not every powerful person operates with positive intent. Some may be Foxes by virtue of their clout, but they're not Foxes in their behavior. They tend *not* to endure. They are so destructive that other people eventually gang up on them, restrain them, and defeat them. It's a fact that sometimes you have to work with people you don't completely trust. Just be careful that when they go down in flames, you're not strapped to their wings.

Control the Environment

The second major benefit for Carol Miller in Bill Thomas's promotion is that she enhances her influence and control at the executive level of the company. At times, Foxes make success look effortless simply because they maneuver so well behind the scenes. But another contributing factor to their

apparently easy victories is that they have shaped their sur-
roundings to the extent that they know exactly which levers
to pull in any situation.

Imagine that, in this company, a critical decision must be
made about development. Everyone agrees on the need to
introduce a certain product, but there is no consensus about
its essential nature and specifications. In fact, there are two
divergent points of view.

One faction is headed by Walter Johnson, the much-admired
vice-president of engineering, who favors the introduction of
a product that will be the most technologically advanced of
its kind, that will seize the high end of the market and stake
the company's claim to an entirely new sector.

In the other camp is marketing. Carol Miller is as aggressive as anyone else about the company's place in the industry,
but she is not persuaded that the product Walter Johnson's
group has in mind is the wisest choice. Carol believes that
going in that direction would dangerously stretch the company
beyond its area of expertise, and that there is equally attractive,
more sensible growth to be gained from offering a product
that is more an extension of the company's existing strength
than a potentially perilous leap into a new business.

The issue must be decided, and it must be resolved at a
meeting of the executive committee. It seems that there is
about an even split on which road to take, and that the president
of the company will have to make the final decision. Imagine
you're at that session. Here is what happens.

Walter Johnson gives a twenty-minute presentation about
the product he's proposing. He has done his homework: it's
a well-thought-out approach, the numbers add up, and his
case is indeed compelling.

The president now gives the floor to Carol Miller, who
begins by saying, "I'm impressed with Walter's proposal. As

usual, he's come up with a tremendously creative idea. As you know, I came here favoring an approach that I admit is quite a bit more conservative. But, more than anything, I want to keep an open mind." Is Carol surrendering? Of course not. For any aggressive person, there is great temptation to engage in head-to-head battles with the opposition. For some, it's *fun* sometimes to go with fists flying into a confrontation and let the chips fall where they may. The problem with this is that you can win the battle and lose the war. The clever fighter, on the other hand, excels at winning with ease, and with as few casualties as possible *on both sides.*

Carol continues with, "I still believe that adopting engineering's proposal isn't the wisest course, but the more I think about it, the more I realize that the major impact might not be on marketing. In many respects, I believe that what we decide may come down to manufacturing considerations, and I'd like to hear what Bill Thomas thinks before I go any further." At this point, there are two things that Bill must *not* do. First, he cannot stand up and say, in effect, "I vote with Carol—after all, she's my mentor." He must be careful to prevent this from being read into anything that he does or says, and that's true in a much larger context than this particular meeting.

From time to time, you may find that one of your best customers, someone you view as a real ally, places an order of some size with one of your competitors. Naturally, you should investigate why this was done. Just keep this possibility in mind: it's poison for someone in an organization to be viewed as being in the hip pocket of a vendor, so there are occasions when it makes the most sense politically to buy something from another supplier. For Bill Thomas, his credibility would instantly evaporate if he were seen as someone who merely parrots Carol Miller's point of view.

The second deadly sin for Bill would be to engage Walter Johnson in predatory fashion. If Carol is trying to win the battle without inflicting needless wounds, Bill mustn't start a bloodbath. Fortunately, Bill has been a good student under the tutelage of a Fox.

"I learn something every time I hear Walt talk," Bill says. "Like Carol, I'm impressed with his proposal. And I find it exciting that we're willing to consider taking on that kind of risk. No matter which product we decide upon, I guarantee that manufacturing can handle it." He then goes over to a flipchart stand and turns to a page of figures he had prepared, saying, "Here's the picture. For Walter's proposal, I think I can keep the added capacity and retooling costs down enough to only need an increase in the operating budget of about 26 percent. Also, the CFO and I have done an analysis, and we were surprised that the first-year impact on revenues would be a decline of only about 13 percent. I know that sounds bad, especially when expenses are going to rise so much, but we really thought it would be worse. The only thing that still troubles me a bit is the impact on delivery. Demand has been so high lately on the existing lines that shipping delays now exceed five weeks. That's becoming a real customer satisfaction problem, and adding another two or three weeks won't help any. We're still working on that one."

Remember, you're a fly on the wall in this meeting. What do you suppose is the look on the CEO's face right about now, as he asks, "Is this pretty much the same for the product Carol wants us to select?"

Bill shakes his head slowly. "Oh, no. We could start building that today, and you'd never know the difference."

Now imagine that you are the CEO. You can go with engineering's risky proposal, spend 26 percent more, make 13 percent less, and add to the delivery problem. Or, you can go with marketing's proposal, and never feel a thing. Which line would you get on?

I know this story sounds a bit contrived, but I wanted to keep it simple. Look what happened here. No one attacked the vice-president of engineering, in fact they complimented him. No one even attacked his idea. They praised it. But softly, gently, and indirectly, they killed it.

You can bet that Carol Miller was certain Bill would hold up his end. You can be sure that she knew what buttons had to be pressed for the president to make the desired decision. A Fox is a walking environmental control system.

Survival

There is a company in Michigan that is one of the largest privately held corporations in America. It is consistently rated among the best managed organizations, and one of the best to sell for. But despite their size, they keep a very, very, low profile.

A couple of years ago, one of their salespeople told me about a discussion that occurred at the company's national sales conference. The chairman of the board had just finished giving his review of an extremely successful year when he opened the floor to questions. The first one came from a bright, eager salesperson. "We have such an exciting story to tell," he began. "Why don't more people know about it? We should be on the cover of *Fortune* every month!" There were a lot of laughs and a number of smiles all around. The chairman paused a moment, and answered this way: "The whale that doesn't spout avoids the harpoon."

There is a wisdom in this statement that every Fox knows, either by nature or by experience. A Fox's inclination to work behind the scenes is more than a matter of being able to keep one's ego in check. It's a decision that, in a sense, can be made mathematically.

Remember John Andrews from Chapter 2? As John's influence began to grow, he had to exert it very discreetly. If he flaunted his power, the positive perception people had of him would suddenly change. In the eyes of many, he wouldn't be perceived as "confident" anymore, he would be seen as *conceited*. Instead of being "astute," he would be *cunning*. He wouldn't be someone who "works well" with people, he'd be one who *uses* them. In short, there is a heavy price to pay for being heavy-handed with influence.

The same challenges exist for Carol Miller, but to a more limited extent. She already holds a senior position in her company. Within her formal domain of marketing, her influence cannot exceed her authority—she has all there is. As long as it's a marketing matter, she can be as visible and direct as she would like. She can issue press releases. She can preside at ribbon-cutting ceremonies. She can appear on the *Today* show. But when she exerts her influence in manufacturing, she is technically out of bounds. No matter how well-intentioned she may be, unless she is very subtle, the organization will not tolerate an incursion into someone else's backyard. There is a not-too-fine line between "influencing" the affairs of others and "meddling," and one stays on the correct side of it by acting in an appropriate manner.

Fox Footprints

Just as people have a range of various personalities, so do Foxes. Some are warm, highly extroverted, and garrulous. Others are more subdued, more clinical, even somewhat aloof.

But no matter what face a Fox puts on for the world, there are some common qualities that these impressive people possess. In organizations, you will always find that they are well-respected. They're the kind of people who are approached for their thoughts on significant matters, even if they're not directly involved in them. When they're waiting for an elevator, people will describe something they're working on, and ask the Fox for his or her thoughts. Instinctively, *people value the way a Fox thinks.*

Because they're so highly regarded, Foxes are well "net-worked." As a result, they're always in the know, and are rarely surprised by events. It's hard to sneak up on a fox in the wild, and it's equally unusual for a human Fox to be unprepared for almost anything that develops in an organization.

Let's examine some very specific qualities that typify Foxes, in terms of how they behave in their environments. Knowing these will help you identify Foxlike behavior more accurately and give you some clues to who is in the Fox's inner circle (the Power Base).

Integrity

For a Fox, there is no gray area when it comes to ethics. It's a binary matter: one either has scruples, or one does not. A slightly padded expense report may not seem like a big deal to many people, but it is to a Fox. For him or her, it is indicative of the extent to which a person is guided by certain principles.

Foxes also are very much oriented toward the long term and as a result, they place great emphasis on things that endure. They believe in this principle: quality lasts. So, given their long-term vision, they look for quality in everything, including people. And quality people are those who not only have integrity, but who *project* integrity, just as Foxes do.

People-Orientation

For a Fox, being people-oriented is as important as being company-oriented. Some are outgoing and sociable, but all are very good at building relationships. Foxes are value-driven, and they know where value comes from—it comes from people. Certainly, there is value in results, in work that is accomplished and projects that are completed. But a Fox knows that *people* do the work, that *people* get the results. A Fox will never lose this perspective.

That insight alone can explain some curious behavior you may observe at work from time to time. For example, a Fox might give high priority to some project that, by any objective measure, should get very little emphasis. This would confuse a lot of people, but the Fox's thinking is clear. The project in question may very well have little significance by itself, but by tackling it, the project team is going to gain valuable experience. The Fox may see that somewhere down the road— perhaps even in a *year* or two—the organization will need that expertise.

Value comes from people, and people grow best when they're challenged. That's why you'll consistently find that Foxes are good delegators. They know that by delegating, they expand their capacity to get results. But they also know that when something is delegated, so too is a certain amount of control. That's why many managers have difficulty delegating. In fact, the more important a task, the harder it is for most managers to assign it to someone else. What worries them is this: "Do I trust someone enough to leave this matter in his or her hands?"

How do you suppose a Fox makes such a determination? Your thoughts probably are heading in this direction: a Fox will delegate to people who have proven themselves. Put it in terms—if you haven't already—of the Power Base Principle: Foxes will delegate important matters to someone whose *value* they *recognize*. This means a Fox will delegate something important to *someone in the Power Base*. So, every time you find out to whom a matter of substance has been delegated, you get a clearer picture of the Power Base of an organization.

Risk Assumption

Just as clever fighters make things look easy, Foxes can be risk-takers who actually appear to be rather conservative. We've all heard the term "calculated risk." Here's what is means to a Fox:

$$\text{RISK} = \text{RESPONSIBILITY} - \text{AUTHORITY}$$

You are at risk in an organization when you accept responsibility to meet some objective, but don't have the authority to marshal all the resources required to pull it off. As we've already discovered, when authority is lacking, influence becomes critical.

How responsible does your company hold you for whether your customer buys your product? Unless you're in a very odd selling environment, the answer is "entirely." Now, within the account, how much authority do you have to make them buy? There should be no exceptions to this one: "none." So, your risk is 100 percent. You have all the responsibility and exactly no authority. Let's look at it from another perspective.

Suppose you've sold your product or service to the customer. How responsible does the customer hold you for whether it does everything it's supposed to? Completely, right? Within your company, how much authority do you have to command all the resources it will take to make the product succeed, now and in the future? A lot of people will answer the last question this way: "very little." I would suggest that, except in rare cases, the correct answer is "none." Remember, we're talking about *authority*. It isn't very often that salespeople have the formal power to direct the efforts of manufacturing personnel, shipping supervisors, and support resources. Once again, you have all the responsibility and none of the authority. As before, your risk is 100 percent.

The good news is that a Fox knows this about you. A Fox knows that you lack formal domain over all the things you will need to ensure success. No matter how good a salesperson you are, no matter how persuasive and knowledgeable about products you may be, a Fox knows that in selecting a vendor he or she assumes a certain amount of risk. That's a given.

Some people are willing to blindly accept risk, and they wonder why they keep getting burned by bad decisions. Foxes work to minimize risk to the greatest degree possible. They are not the kind of people who will put up the deed to a house for a five-dollar wager. The way they minimize risk is to manage it. We've all heard the term "managing risk," too. Graphically, Figure 3.2 shows how Foxes do it.

So, knowing that authority is out of the question, what do you suppose a Fox will want to see that you have? You got it—influence. Despite your lack of authority, when you can demonstrate to a Fox that you have influence—that you are sufficiently "connected" within your own organization to make

Figure 3.2. Risk management.

things happen—you represent real value, because your influence diminishes the Fox's risk.

A Fox in the Mirror

In your sales efforts, everything you do must reflect integrity. When a Fox sees, in you, a high-quality person who shares his or her values, you will gain access to a source of considerable clout, perhaps even becoming part of the Power Base yourself, at least as it relates to some issues.

Every time anything worthwhile is to be done in an organization, there is risk. Foxes are willing to accept risk, but only an amount acceptable in comparison to the value of the endeavor, and only when the risk can be driven down by working with people who project integrity and who represent real added value. When that happens, when a Fox sees that working with you decreases his or her risk, your risk goes down, too—your risk of not getting the business. In this way, you, like the Fox, are managing risk. It puts you on the inside, in a position of competing from within. Once you're there, some remarkable things can happen for you.

Chapter 4

Competing from Within: How to Develop Sales Opportunities

The good general cultivates resources.
—Sun Tzu

Among the talents of Ivy League street fighters is the ability to create demand, not only to respond to sales opportunities, but to actually *develop* those opportunities. A critical factor in creating demand is the ability to provide a higher degree of added value than is customary in a sales campaign.

Although the value associated with a product is quite real, it has a very limited effect in terms of producing competitive advantage. That is why most salespeople quickly learn to link their product's capabilities to the solution of a pressing business concern of the customer's. Nevertheless, contrary to popular belief, business value is not the top rung of the ladder, and doesn't necessarily create demand, at least for *you*. You have much more to offer people in an account, value that can make you virtually immune from competitive threat in the right situations.

The only way to create demand for yourself, to the exclusion of all others, is to help key people do *for* themselves what they cannot do *by* themselves. If whatever product or service you offer has value, and if you can also bring business value to the table, you will develop an irresistible source of competitive advantage when you add *political value* to the equation.

At the end of Chapter 2, I asked you to think back to the beginning of the John Andrews story, to a point before all the good things happened for him, before the selection of a vendor had been made. I left it with this question: what if John hadn't been so sharp, hadn't realized the political potential that rested in the project he had been assigned, had been unaware of the prospect of a new department being created, and hadn't had much insight into Fred Pearson's values?

I suggested that if you could fill that void, you would greatly increase your potential to win. If you can provide the political value to Andrews of bridging the gap between what he doesn't know *by* himself and can't do *for* himself, you will suddenly find yourself on the inside, looking out at your opponents tapping on the glass.

Your competition will approach this sales situation very traditionally. John Andrews is the decision maker, so they will lock in on him. They will try to be very persuasive when telling their product's story; the better they are, the more they will show John compelling business reasons to go with them, perhaps on the basis of financial benefits, company reputation, or a terrific support plan. The more experienced they are, the more formidable they will be.

Top-Down Street Fighting

You may be able to go in and slug it out with the best of them, but remember, the clever fighter excels at winning with ease.

You, too, will get to John Andrews, but you won't lock on to him until you can put him in better perspective.

In electronic intelligence gathering, one of the biggest challenges (besides code breaking) is distinguishing signals from noise. In a sales situation, until you get some fix on the informal structure of the organization, a peek behind the scenes into the Power Base, you can't pick up the political significance of what's going on. Who's influencing whom, what people's political aspirations are, what really needs to be accomplished, and what's important in how it gets accomplished—all of this represents information communicated to people who have relationships with others who are in the Power Base. So to put John Andrews into perspective, politically, you need to understand the political environment. Building associations with the Power Base provides you with the decoding ability necessary to separate what looks like noise to your competition from politically significant data. But where are the signals coming from?

For any important matter, the person sending out the signals will be the Fox. To calibrate the significance of a project and to get an accurate picture of what's important to the person calling the plays, you've got to go to the source, as early in the sales campaign as possible.

In this case, it's Fred Pearson. As soon as you refine your view of the political structure of this organization, you'll see Fox footprints everywhere he walks.

Gaining access to senior managers such as Fred is a challenge for everyone. The reason a lot of people don't succeed at it—and why many never even try—is very simple: the only language understood by most salespeople, that of product value, isn't spoken at senior levels.

In the beginning, connecting with someone on Pearson's level for anything more than a one-time contact will be completely determined by whether Fred senses that there is potential business value in opening a dialogue with you. He must conclude that you are more than a product representative, that you are someone whose primary focus is on *his* company's business rather than on *your* company's product.

To maintain the contact, to develop a relationship, your value must increase. Very early, Fred must perceive the political value of you as a resource to help him get things done that he *wants* done, and in the *way* he wants them done.

Every executive, from the president of the United States to the CEO of a small company, needs an informal network to ensure that formal directives are carried out. Everyone in a senior position has experienced the frustration of having directives forgotten, ignored, or watered down to the point of insignificance. They know that to really make things happen, they have to cultivate resources.

As soon as you establish credibility with someone like Fred Pearson, you become a resource to be cultivated, and you develop a link to John Andrews that has some muscle behind it. Your relationship with a Fox gives you an entry into the informal aspects of an account that most of your competitors will never know.

By the way, Fred won't be confused about your motives. He knows that eventually you'll want to sell your product. His attraction to qualities he sees in you will be based on the fact that you're going about your work in the right context.

Whenever there is a major investment at stake in a buying decision, your job is more than a matter of selling a product. Because there's a lot on the line, what you're really doing is influencing an organization. Careers are made and broken by major decisions, so there is always a political component in a sales situation.

In one respect, you help people just by offering a good product. But in a much deeper sense, you have a role in the protection of their positions and the advancement of their ambitions. Whether you fulfill your role passively or *manage* it actively is entirely in your hands.

Fred Pearson certainly knows your role, and as soon as he believes that you know it, and are competent to work within the political structure, you will be granted special privileges and information that aren't granted to others.

If it will help Fred to have someone like you "in the know" about his plans for expanding the organization, he'll clue you in. He will share his perspective and values about the project that's underway so that you can promote them at the operations level. And, he will tell you an awful lot about John Andrews.

Fred is thinking about creating a new department within the next several months, and he knows that Andrews is ambitious. It doesn't take a genius to put two and two together and see that an opportunity exists for John, but Andrews may not know about the new department, and as a result, may miss the opportunity.

Senior managers don't wait until the last minute to decide who to put in an important position. Well before Fred Pearson reorganizes his division, he will employ a kind of value seeking sonar.

Sound waves bouncing off the hull of a ship come back to the sender in the form of "pings." By calibrating them, the location, size, and course of another vessel can be fixed. In fact, warships are equipped with devices to alert them to when they're being pinged.

John Andrews may not have that capability. He may not know that he's being pinged to determine whether he has the "size" for the job. He may not know what course he must set, in terms of his approach to the task at hand, to become a viable candidate for promotion.

From your association with the Fox, you can provide political value to John Andrews, and you're ready to deal with him in the sales situation from an insider's position of knowledge and strength.

Word spreads fast in organizations, and you can be sure that John knows about your dialogue with Fred. In fact, the first thing you may have to deal with in working with John is a certain wariness about you on his part.

So, as you begin interacting with him, your approach is rather conventional. You state your understanding of the company's needs, and express in general terms your proposal for meeting them. You describe your product's capabilities, emphasizing benefits all along the way.

But, at the appropriate point, at an off-line moment—perhaps after the meeting is officially over—you begin to stake out the inside track. You casually ask John for his insight about the importance of the project he's working on. This leads you into a brief conversation about where he sees, in general, the organization going.

From there, the next question is natural: where does John see *himself* going? His answer—that he would like to advance in the company—represents his *personal agenda*.

The essence of providing political value is advancing the personal agenda of a key person like John Andrews. We're going to get into the mechanics of making this kind of contribution in Chapter 11. For now, we need only focus on the outcomes you desire and the manner in which you must go about achieving them.

In the previous chapter, I mentioned that Carol Miller's involvement in the manufacturing department had to be discreet because she had no formal authority there. The same principle applies in your dealings with John Andrews.

Technically, you have no business being John Andrews' career counselor, and in point of fact, that's not the role you will play. But remember, everything he does in the course of the project will affect his career. He's being pinged. All you want to do is communicate that you're aware of that, make him aware of it, and let him know that you're there to help him.

You accomplish all of this informally and casually. You find opportunities to share the special insight you gained from Fred Pearson. Naturally, you don't violate any confidences that Pearson may have shared with you, but you indirectly help John understand some of the larger issues, particularly as they relate to the possible creation of a new department, and specifically as they relate to Fred Pearson's desires.

Because you're politically connected in his company, John will quickly realize that you represent political value to him. As this becomes clear, John will see you not only as a salesperson, but as an extension of Fred Pearson—the individual he most needs for his personal agenda to be fulfilled. The Power Base Principle begins to work for you the moment John senses that you can help make it work for him.

By basing your sales efforts on signals from Fred Pearson, you have become a conduit for his expectations, and John knows that the pipeline flows in both directions. As much as you are a link from Fred to John, you also serve as a connection the other way, a medium for the right pings to go back to the executive suite.

Back to the Future

As we conclude the adventures of John Andrews, you will recall that eventually he was promoted, and now heads the new department that was created (see Figure 2.1). Moving ahead another year, John's performance has proved that Fred

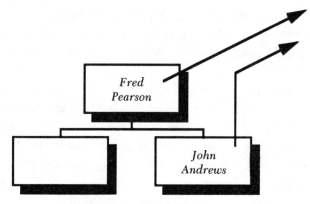

Figure 4.1. The drafting process.

Pearson made the right choice. But now, there's another change in the organization: Pearson resigns.

Fred accepts a position as executive vice-president with a start-up company. He gets an equity position and the chance he's long dreamed of: to be on the vanguard of a dynamic new company in a potentially explosive industry.

When this happens to the Fred Pearsons of the world, what often becomes of the John Andrews? It's called "drafting," as seen in Figure 4.1

From day one in his new job, no matter how senior he is, a process will begin for Fred Pearson: every move he makes will be scrutinized. He will be pinged. It's not that the board of directors feels that Fred has to be supervised, it's simply that management at any level always wants to be sure that someone they've brought into the company contributes something to the organization: value.

Fred is in an important position in this company, so it is critical that he provides value. His first few months on the job will have a significant impact on his future success. In that time, he'll need to set the direction for his organization, stake his claim to leadership, and get moving.

To do those things, he'll need help. When you need help, who do you call for? You call for people you know can help you, people who have proven themselves in the past. That's why drafting occurs, and why the bond between a Pearson and an Andrews is so often a long-term proposition. It's a matter of cultivating resources.

When your value matures from that of a product representative and a business resource to a political ally, the drafting process will work for you, too. Way back when John Andrews first perceived political value in working with you and made his buying decision in large part because of it, your draft status became 1-A—but this is the kind of draft you'll like. When John was promoted to head the new department, you got a promotion, too.

Just as Fred Pearson will surround himself with key resources that have contributed to his success, so will anyone in John Andrews' place. A mutual bond forms between you and John. To the degree it is practical, he will protect you, and insulate you from competitive threat. After all, you're valuable to John, and as with anyone, he will protect what he values.

If you've ever been in a sales situation where you sense that a competitor is shaping the buying criteria, perhaps even ghostwriting the Request for Proposal (RFP), you're going up against a vendor who is being insulated in this fashion. If you've ever been in those happy circumstances yourself, you know the safety and strength that can be found when you're competing from within, cultivating resources.

If you have product value in a situation where there also is business value for the customer in making an acquisition, you *may* win. If these two conditions exist, and if there is compelling political value in working with you, you *will* win.

As you decide who you can assist in this manner, and begin to structure your actual contribution, you will be forming a political strategy for an account that is separate and distinct from your formal, business-related efforts. This is a challenging aspect of sales strategy, one whose mechanics cannot be adequately addressed until we explore the essence of strategy itself.

Part Two: Engaging the Competition

Chapter 5

The Direct Strategy: Making a Frontal Assault on the Competition

---

The truly wise can perceive things before they have come to pass.

—Sun Tzu

The Four Strategies: An Overview

Because selling is a process of competing for business, to be ready to sell, you must be ready to compete. Competitive readiness is a state of preparation and when you attain it, you have done more than simply schedule time to make sales calls. When you are competitive-ready, you are prepared and able to engage the competition in the battle for business and defeat them with swiftness, agility, and a minimal expenditure of resources. It is a manner of operating that is governed by the will to prepare to win, and is the trademark of Ivy League street fighters.

You are not necessarily competitive-ready simply because you are already competing. Although you may be active in a selling effort, you can't be sure that you're active in the right way—doing the right things, employing the right tactics at the right time—until you make a more fundamental determination about the sales strategy you will rely upon for success.

A strategy is a central, organizing statement that allows you to make good decisions about what you'll do in a sales campaign. Every tactic—everything you physically do—must advance a vision of what it's going to take to win. Over the next four chapters, we're going to explore a way to gain that kind of vision. You'll learn to look at every sales opportunity through a window, a structure that helps you understand exactly what *kind* of strategy you must employ to be successful. This "window of opportunity" consists of four panes of glass—each one representing a class of strategy—listed below. For every sales opportunity, one class of strategy—one of the four panes—will characterize your best approach to winning the business.

- At times, you'll have the strength to implement a *direct* challenge to the competition.
- On occasion, you'll have to take a more *indirect* path, changing the ground rules on the leaders and pulling the rug out from under them.
- At other times, you'll need a more limited *divisional* approach, where you'll "divide and conquer" the competition to secure a piece of business you can't win by other means, or to gain access to an account peacefully and quietly, so you can build for the future.

- Given the choice between a loss and a no-decision, there will be times when a *containment* strategy is your best approach to a sales situation, slowing down the sales cycle long enough to gain or regain your strength.

As we examine these four classes of strategy in this and the next three chapters, we'll address conditions that must exist for each one to succeed, as well as circumstances where you would be wise to select a different approach. When you understand the strengths and weaknesses of each kind of strategy, you will be able to make rapid decisions about what *must* transpire in the sales cycle for you to win, well before it comes to pass. At that point, deciding what tactics to use, and in what sequence, will be a natural, sensible, and creative process, and the impact of each tactic will have maximum effect.

A Frontal Assault

By far, the most common strategy employed in selling is a *direct approach*. With it, you go head-to-head against the competition, trying to match your strength against theirs. In fact, you're trying to overmatch them. Using a direct approach implies that you have the muscle to simply knock down any obstacles you encounter.

Without question, there are times when a direct strategy is appropriate in selling. But you should think very carefully before selecting it as the essence of your sales campaign. This is true for the other classes, too, but I emphasize it here because a direct approach is the *only* kind of strategy most people know how to use.

The direct strategy is attractive because it is uncomplicated, no matter how difficult a sales situation may be. After all, just as the shortest distance between two points is a straight line, the straightest path to meeting a sales objective would seem to be to make your product's features and benefits look more appealing than that of the competition's. That's one reason most people default to a direct approach. Another is because they honestly believe it's the only way to win business. For them, the selling process is very basic: if the customer believes you have the best product or service, you'll win. If the customer doesn't, you'll lose. By that reasoning, in order to win you simply *must* prove that you have the superior product offering. The problem with that logic is if you *don't* have that superiority. Or, if all things are pretty much even. Or, even worse, if your product is actually deficient in some areas. Does this mean you are destined to lose?

No Ivy League street fighter worth his or her salt would accept that. He or she would realize that when you don't have superiority, it simply means the direct approach isn't the way to go. You have to go to the window of opportunity, look through the other panes of glass, and find the one that will "click" for you. One of them will instantly appear as the road to victory, while the direct approach would have led either to defeat or to a long, protracted, laborious struggle for an uncertain result.

That's my cautionary note on automatically going head-to-head against the competition. Remember, your purpose as a salesperson is not simply to sell, but to win. With that in mind, let's look at three specific variations of a direct strategy. While you shouldn't mindlessly go direct in every sales situation, circumstances will arise when you *will* have enough strength to blow away the competition, and you should take full advantage of those opportunities. It will help you to know exactly what sources of strength you may be able to draw upon.

Variation One: Product Superiority

If a company has a somewhat unique offering it may be able to use a direct strategy with impunity on a grand, corporate scale. Wherever there's a rock-solid need for a product that only one vendor can supply, that vendor has a fairly high degree of built-in competitive advantage. As other firms enter the market, they must first overcome the brand name identity the industry leader enjoys.

As a rule, companies don't like to have their names become generic terms. As much as Coca-Cola wants you to order a "Coke," they don't want you to do so and then be served a Pepsi. The people at Kleenex don't want that name automatically applied to all facial tissues, and obviously won't allow it when it comes to competitors' products. The Xerox Corporation isn't wildly happy when people refer to making "xeroxes" on a Savin photocopier.

A company's name slips into general usage, though, because at some point and for some time its products, such as Coke, Kleenex, and Xerox, are seen as having exclusive ownership of the market. It may only be a matter of perception, but the fact remains that, while the perception exists, those companies enjoy an enormous competitive advantage. There's no product superiority like being the only game in town, and a company can leverage it to the hilt in a very direct way. Eventually, of course, other vendors catch up. The distinctions between competitive offerings begin to blur, and industry leaders have to make adjustments to their strategy. But on rare occasion, a company locks up product superiority to such a degree that they can remain in a direct mode for decades.

In 1949, Dr. Edwin Land invented a process for instant photography and formed the Polaroid Corporation. As remarkable as was his technological breakthrough, even more impressive was the extent and completeness to which he was able to impenetrably patent the process. Over the better part of four decades, no other company has been able to successfully enter the instant photography field. Kodak tried, and its reward was to suffer a court judgment in an infringement suit brought by Polaroid that cost the company dearly in rebates and damages.

Few salespeople represent products that have no competition, and I'd bet that no Polaroid salesperson would say that he or she does not work in a competitive environment. The company certainly must compete in the larger market for films and cameras with other formats and technologies. But in their basic business they stand alone; in a sense they only compete with themselves to make each new product evolutionary and superior in contrast to its predecessors. Even if your own company doesn't have such unquestioned preeminence, the products you offer may virtually blow away the competition in terms of capabilities or performance. As a result, you may be able to win a great deal of business based only on that overwhelming strength, at least until the competition catches up, which they usually do. Just beware of one of the facts of life in selling: a good product is not necessarily a superior product. Even a very good product may not yield the kind of superiority that will give you a decided edge in a sales situation, to the degree that you could run a direct strategy centered around it.

If you employ a direct strategy when your product really isn't perceived by the customer as superior, you are essentially deciding to meet your competition on a level playing field. That's very sporting of you, but it might be tantamount to surrender. Even worse, when an objective analysis shows that your product is actually weaker than the competition's, it would be even more unwise to default to a direct mode, fighting features battles you have little or no chance of winning. You'd be surprised at how many salespeople try exactly that approach, and you would be amused to know how many of them are mystified when it leads to defeat.

Consider this variation of the direct strategy only when *you're absolutely convinced* that your product's strengths will overwhelm the competition. If you're not convinced, you have alternatives. But even before you consider another class of strategy entirely, there are a couple of other ways to employ a direct approach.

Variation Two: Selling the Company

In the early days of the computer industry, the hands-down market leader was the Univac division of Sperry Rand, a company that had a huge lead in technology going into the late 1940s. Naturally, their strategy was a direct one based on product superiority at that time. There weren't a lot of computer users in those days, and fewer still who had technological expertise. Buyers were highly dependent on awe-inspiring product wizards, and Univac had an abundant supply of them. As a result, a Univac sales call often more closely resembled a graduate seminar in computer sciences than the "solutions sell" that is typical in the industry today. But the company was viewed in many quarters as the only game in town, and for a while, it *was* dominant.

Univac did have a competitor, however, by the name of International Business Machines, which was decidedly in the catch-up mode from a product point of view. To be competitive, IBM took a different tack in their sales effort and found a weakness in Univac they could exploit. In the process, IBM began implementing a form of the direct strategy that they still capitalize upon to this day—it's called "selling the company."

The IBM sales approach wasn't aimed to astound and amaze customers with technological wonderment. In fact, even though the company's training of commercial salespeople covered essential product knowledge, it focused mainly on the business issues of the industries in which salespeople would be operating. Marketing reps were taught that executives in their accounts were much more interested in saving money and speeding up operations than they were in circuitry and data paths. At the same time, the IBM's management fostered an intense dedication to service and support. While horror stories abounded of Univac system failures that left customers high and dry, IBM became legendary for descending en masse on problem installations with swarms of marketing, support, and technical personnel—from executives on down—all brandishing soldering irons.

The net was an opening for IBM salespeople to win business. As long as they could be within range on product issues they could achieve superiority (and competitive advantage) in other ways. With their business-oriented approach they were speaking their customers' language. With their company's growing reputation as one that would stand by its customers, they could de-emphasize the product, and thus diminish the impact of any technical superiority a Univac system may possess. In short, they could make the central buying decision center around which company the customers perceived would be the best one to do business with.

All this time, Univac continued to make technological advances, but more and more buyers selected IBM. In fact, in a one-year period in the mid-1950s, Univac's market share of large computers fell over 30 percent, virtually all of its loss having been suffered at the hands of IBM. For their part, the success of IBM, or "Big Blue," as it is nicknamed, exploded in this period to the extent that they captured a staggering 84.9 percent of the total domestic market for computers of all sizes. "Selling the company" became the hallmark of IBM's marketing strategy, and remains so today. Every now and then, a classic set of IBM print ads run in newspapers and magazines around the world. They're very simple. All you see is a pillow, and underneath it these words: "With IBM, you never have to worry about getting a good night's sleep."

A sales campaign that focuses more on which *company* customers should buy from, as opposed to which *product* they should buy, represents a distinctly direct approach. When you use it, your aim is to blow away the competition not on product issues, but on larger ones.

Imagine you're in a situation where the major vendors all offer very similar products. Also, their pricing structures are essentially identical. But suppose your company is the hands-down industry leader. You're a household name, you have a reputation for high-quality products and for standing by the customer. This strength may allow you to capitalize on your firm's reputation with a direct approach of "selling the company." In every sales call you make, you'll grant that product and price are important considerations, and you'll state the benefits you offer in those areas. But also you will take every opportunity to remind the customer that buying from the right company should be the most important consideration. You'll emphasize the wisdom of buying from a vendor who has experience, who is established in the industry, and who is stable enough to make customers confident that the company will be there, years later, to support them.

As with product superiority, the important thing to keep in mind when considering whether to use this variation of the direct strategy is if your company reputation is perceived as truly superior. As before, there's a big difference between having a good reputation and having such extraordinary fame that you have a significant advantage. For this kind of direct strategy to work, you have to prove that you are clearly superior in terms of your company's ability to solve the kind of problems your customer is facing, and that you can do so significantly better than any of your competitors.

Variation Three: Product Linking

A third derivative of the direct strategy involves situations where you already have a strong presence in an account. As new sales opportunities arise with the customer, you may be able to gain competitive advantage simply because of the strength of your installation, even if your products have begun to lag somewhat in sophistication and capabilities.

If you own a videocassette recorder, the odds are it's a VHS format machine. Now, imagine that you decide to buy a second VCR, one to hook up to the television in your bedroom. When you go to your local customer electronics store, you find a VCR at a very good price that has some great new features. There's only one problem: it works in the Beta format. You can buy this machine at a great price and get those terrific features, but you won't be able to use it to watch all the videotapes you already own.

If you're like most people, you wouldn't buy this unit. Instead, you'd buy another VHS deck—even if its price may be a little higher—because the incompatibility between VHS tapes and a Beta deck defeats the purpose of convenience that set you on the buying path to begin with. There's a link between the product you'll buy and the one you already have.

Beyond convenience, most business customers want to achieve a fairly high level of stability from the products and services they acquire from vendors. They want these products, in effect, to become invisible—to become such a normal, integral, and effortless part of their operation that they do not distract attention from the demands of business. So here you are, the incumbent vendor, and your customer is about to make an acquisition to expand their installation. Unless a competitor's product will be fully compatible with what you've already installed, with no cost to the customer in terms of conversion or retraining, you have a built-in advantage and can go direct by linking the buying decision to your existing installed base. All the tangibles are working in your favor.

You also have intangible factors working for you. Even if an account is considering bringing in a niche vendor to solve a specific problem, the customer will be working with you on the bigger issues in the future. That's an important relationship, one the customer is equally responsible with you to protect. Senior managers in companies today more and more often recognize how the quality of their products can be improved by working with as few vendors as possible, and to establish strong relationships with the ones they rely upon. As long as your company markets a range and line of products that will serve disparate needs, you have a situation where your product mix will allow you to virtually own an account as it applies to the kind of solutions you have to offer.

In one of your accounts, if your company has been the established supplier for some time, and if no other company can offer a product that is compatible—and if this is critical to the customer—the choice for your strategy in new sales opportunities with them would very likely be the product linking variation of the direct approach. In all of your efforts, you would address the decision makers' expressed needs, but would also emphasize the positive aspects of "staying the course." From time to time, you would gently bring up the prospect of a disruption in the customer's operation should another vendor be brought in.

Two things must be true for this version of the direct strategy to work for you. The first one is obvious: the customer must be satisfied with the product or service they've already received from you. After all, linking your sales efforts to a failed installation is roughly equivalent to celebrating having survived the Chicago fire by taking a cruise on the Titanic. The second requirement is that customers must conclude, perhaps reluctantly, that their attraction to another supplier isn't worth the drawbacks of having a multi-vendor environment. If it's a toss-up, your presence in the account shouldn't lull you into thinking you have an edge.

The View through the Glass

The main requirement for the direct strategy is clear superiority, either from product, reputation, installed base, or any combination thereof, from the customer's point of view. Without it, implementing a direct approach could be a grievous error, one that some of the largest companies in America have committed. Here are some examples.

In 1983, IBM decided that their product superiority in personal computers would give them a clear shot at the home computer market. They introduced a machine called the PC jr., priced it too high for the computer novice, and made it too limited in capability for the initiated. The product failed to meet expectations and was discontinued two years later.

In 1985, Coca-Cola believed that sales would invigorate with a sweeter reformulation of Coke, and that the company's name alone would carry the new product so well that they could discontinue their traditional product. You know the rest of the story.

In 1984, Federal Express tried, with ZapMail, to product-link their overnight pickup and delivery business to a new service. They proposed to pick up customers' documents and fax them to another Federal Express office for local delivery. Customers sensibly saw the advantages of simply buying their own fax machines. ZapMail went away, taking $233 million of Federal Express's money with it.

A strategy that doesn't conform to the test of common sense is no strategy at all—it's a whim. If you can't look at a sales opportunity through the window and see some source of clear superiority, you shouldn't implement a direct strategy. The rules don't favor you, and whenever that's the case, you shouldn't play the game. A change in the rules may be called for.

Chapter 6

The Indirect Strategy: Pulling the Rug out from under the Competition

Appear where you are not expected.
—Sun Tzu

I f nothing about your product, company, or installed base gives you an edge over the competition, you probably should not try a direct strategy. If you do, you're only saving the competition from having to weaken you, because you're doing it to yourself. More importantly, if your objective analysis shows that you're actually weaker than the competition, you *definitely* should not try a direct strategy. David and Goliath is a great story, but when was the last time you saw a giant felled by a slingshot? You do have alternatives, and the *indirect* approach is the first one you should consider.

Ground Rules Can Be Changed

An indirect strategy is used when you conclude that you cannot succeed on the field of battle as it is currently defined. With an indirect approach, you work to change the ground rules by which the decision is to be made. Think about the American Revolution, and what the rules were going to be from a British point of view. For them, the conflict would be waged according to custom. Well-trained, immaculately uniformed troops from both sides would make a broad-daylight march in precise columns to an open field. Pipes and drums would play the ancient tunes of battle, as both sides assumed their formations. Officers wearing plumed hats, sabers in hand, would pace behind the lines of troops, barking orders. It would be an orderly affair. After soldiers in one row fired, they would reload from a crouch to allow troops behind them a clear shot at the enemy. At the end, whichever side's troops were breathing the best and bleeding the least would be the winner.

It didn't take the colonials too long to figure out that, for them, these terms of battle were not exactly favorable. Unless the weather was particularly fine, they couldn't muster all that many soldiers. They didn't have the wherewithal to procure attractive uniforms or vast quantities of ammunition—not to mention musical instruments. Nevertheless, they wanted their liberty, so they quickly decided that a change in the ground rules was called for. Against superior numbers, daylight is not your friend, so the colonials attacked at night whenever possible. They decided not to fight in the open fields, but to ambush the British from behind rocks and trees. This actually produced an advantage from their embarrassing shortage of uniforms—they could employ guerrilla tactics, hitting quickly and then fading away into the local populace. They were safe there; many civilians were Tories, so the British couldn't just round them all up to get at a few pesky revolutionaries. As we all know from our history, when the ground rules changed, the outcome changed. It works the same way in business.

Marketing Applications of the Indirect Strategy

A lot has changed in recent years for the fashion company Gucci, but it has always been known as one of the most exclusive producers of luxury accessories in the world. They had decided to play—and win—by a different set of rules from those observed by their competitors.

Imagine that you run a worldwide company that makes fine leather goods. Suddenly, one of your products becomes tremendously popular. Sales are going through the roof. What do you do? Well, if you play by normal marketing rules, you try to make sure that you get the best ride you can from this wave. Elasticity of demand is working in your favor, so you may increase the price of the product. You'll definitely ramp up production. In other words, you'll milk the product for everything its worth, for as long as you can.

Gucci has always answered to the beat of a different drum. When one of its products became very popular, when it really started to sell like hotcakes, Gucci discontinued it. It would be gone. Off the shelf. Forever.

Gucci's founders knew what business they were in. They knew they weren't in the handbag business, or the shoe business, or the leather goods business. They knew they were in the fashion business, and that part of their allure was their exclusivity. They didn't want just anyone carrying Gucci bags, nor everyone carrying the same one. They also wanted to create a certain effect when people came in to a Gucci shop just to browse.

Suppose, for example you're on a Caribbean vacation and have stopped by the local Gucci store on the main street of one of the islands. You see a briefcase that you fall in love with but it costs $700 (making it an *attaché* case), so you decide to think about it. In fact, you think about it after you get home, and for the next few months. Every now and then, you see someone carrying the briefcase you had your eye on. So, when you get a nice bonus check, you decide to run down to your local Gucci dealer and buy one for yourself. You get your first piece of bad news when you don't see the briefcase you covet on display. You get the second dose when you're informed that the dealer doesn't have it in stock. The crushing blow comes when the clerk tells you that Gucci has discontinued that particular item.

Now, the next time you're in a Gucci shop and you get the impulse to buy something that attracts you, what will you do? Buy it, of course. Gucci's strategy made the impulse buy a very rational decision for consumers, all because Gucci played by a different set of rules, augmenting normal buying criteria by including the prospect of scarcity.

Now, let's look at another example. Several years ago, a few enterprising people believed that the dolls they made by hand in their home, which their friends and family loved so much, might be attractive to the general public. So they decided to form a small company. Nothing big was ever planned, but they definitely were going into the doll-making business. Now the ground rules for this industry had been in place for quite some time. Dolls were pretty and cute, priced low enough to sell, and for the most part differentiated by features that replicated this or that biological function of real children. But the makers of this new entry to the market—later to be called Cabbage Patch Kids dolls—knew they couldn't compete on that playing field. Knowingly or unknowingly, they couldn't match the major toy manufacturers in marketing, distribution, or economies of scale. To be successful, a change in the ground rules was absolutely essential.

I'm sure you remember the craze for Cabbage Patch Kids dolls. The dolls still sell fairly well. Almost everything about these dolls is different. Cabbage Patch Kids dolls aren't pretty—in fact, they are homely, even ugly. They aren't easy on the pocketbook, either, and were extremely expensive when they were first introduced. But people lined up at stores when a new supply was in, willing to pay almost any price, and the dolls sold out almost instantly. No one wanted to miss his or her chance—the Gucci effect all over again—especially just before the holidays. You see, dolls had traditionally been sold as toys. Those were the ground rules of the industry. But Cabbage Patch Dolls weren't sold as toys. They were positioned as *companions*. A $100 toy may seem expensive, but it's a small price to pay for companionship, isn't it? In fact, from the company's point of view, Cabbage Patch Kids dolls weren't *bought*; they were "adopted."

Before they came to be mass-produced by Coleco (and this is, to some extent, still true today), Cabbage Patch Kids dolls were made to perpetuate this fundamentally different view of a child's product. For example, each doll had a name and even a birth certificate. Stitching on the dolls was randomly changed by computer to create uniqueness. Children could send their Cabbage Patch Kids dolls to camp—literally—and receive letters from them while they were away.

By the way, there's a maxim in strategic planning that you stay with a given strategy unless conditions dramatically change. When you adhere to this principle, you don't get confused. You stay, being both efficient and effective, on the one road you decided is best to take you to your objective. Of course, you can only apply this principle when you thoroughly think through and reality-test a strategy you're considering. When conditions changed for Cabbage Patch Kids dolls, that is, when they became tremendously successful, the company decided it was appropriate to change strategies. They went direct, by product linking. After the initial burst of volume, sales add-on's for Cabbage Patch Kids dolls were even more profitable than the dolls themselves. After all, why buy kids just another toy when you can buy clothes, or a buggy, or what have you for the doll they already have?

To a lot of people, the Cabbage Patch Kids phenomenon seemed bizarre. But from a strategic point of view, it made perfect sense. If the original makers of Cabbage Patch Kids really wanted to make a go at a business, they had to find a differentiation that customers would value, and that their company could uniquely provide. That was the only way they could effectively compete; without the differentiating factors, the odds against success would have been insurmountable.

When you're out-numbered and out-gunned in a sales situation, you need to find your own way to change the field of battle. At times, it will take some real creativity and hard work. But using your imagination and applying a bit of elbow grease is infinitely preferable to getting hammered by the competition.

Sales Applications of the Indirect Strategy

Let's say you're in banking, and that you sell financial services to middle-market companies. In fact, you specialize in selling commercial loans. The customary ground rules for this kind of business aren't terribly complex. Customers tend to borrow funds from institutions where they can get the best interest rate and the most favorable terms on collateral requirements. Banking is a highly regulated industry, so, as you can imagine, there isn't a great deal of differentiation you would have to offer in your selling efforts. At least not on the traditional field of battle.

It's important to note here that this is exactly the kind of sale, a so-called "commodity" business, where salespeople often employ a direct approach even though they don't have clear superiority in product, reputation, or an established relationship. As a result, the sales effort tends to degenerate into a "personality" sell. The theory is that, when all things are equal, people will buy from people they like. So, selling becomes only a matter of being friendly, of cozying up to a prospective customer, of being his or her buddy. One problem with this approach is that having a customer like you really is effective only if he or she happens to dislike your competitor. The other problem is that in the absence of major differentiation, minor factors become the elements that determine a decision. A marginally lower price may win the day for one vendor, while an insignificant product feature may tip the scales for another. In our banking scenario, a competitor's point off the interest rate for a loan, or more lenient collateral policy, puts you behind the eight ball.

When you don't have a major differentiation, when you don't have clear superiority, you shouldn't go direct. The ground rules are either working against you or at least aren't giving you an edge. You have to change them. You have to *create* differentiation. You have to make your own Cabbage Patch Doll.

As an example, maybe your simple strategy statement in one of those accounts where there's a prospect for commercial loan business would read like this: "Change the ground rules away from being the lowest cost source of capital to that of providing a total business package based on a lasting business relationship." You'll still have to offer the customer a solid package on the interest rate and collateral, but you won't necessarily have to offer the best deal in those respects. Your strategy suggests that the customary factors are not what you're relying upon for success. And while your competitors are slugging it out in a very predictable way, with big smiles and "happy face" stickers, you'll be showing the customer a bigger picture. Your tactics will have to make the strategy come to life.

One tactic may be to offer the customer's employees free checking accounts at your bank. Maybe you'll arrange for them to get a preferred rate on personal loans, as well. The key is to offer a total package. With a clear sense of strategy, you can become very creative. Perhaps your bank uses a PC-based system that tracks accounts, maturation of securities, and the like. It may occur to you that your customer would benefit (or perceive they would benefit) by having access to the same system. If you can arrange it, you've instantly set yourself off from the rest of the pack.

The point is, every tactic, everything you do, will be aimed at establishing the clear advantage in the customer's mind of developing a lasting business relationship with you and your bank. That's the strategy. If the value is real, and if it is recognized (the Power Base Principle applied in a slightly different way), you will shift the buying criteria onto turf where you stand head and shoulders above your competition.

Of course, financial considerations are always a factor. This particular sales strategy wouldn't work for a banker selling to an account that was extremely price sensitive, where the only issue was the bottom line and nothing, but nothing, else mattered. Selecting the right strategy is a function of getting insight about the particular nature of each account and each sales situation. For example, you may often find you have to use an indirect strategy to diminish the impact of price when yours is significantly higher than another vendor's. Suppose you have a customer who is really driving the decision based on the bottom line. Product capabilities or service features are pretty much standard among you and other vendors, but one company is offering a ridiculously low price that you can't match. They're new in your industry, and just want to get a foot in the door of this account to begin building an installed base.

Once you rule out a direct strategy because of a lack of superiority, you would be wise to start looking for ways to alter the buying criteria. Perhaps an area where your company excels, but where this competitor is weak because they're so new, is in "ongoing support." This may represent just the opportunity you're looking for. To win, your strategy may have to be "to change the central buying criterion from price to ongoing support," and every tactic you employ will have to help make that important to the customer. Naturally, the buyer isn't going to simply abandon his or her desire for a cost-effective product. You'll still have to deal with financial issues. For you, what's most important is that you effect a shift in the customer's emphasis and priorities. An indirect strategy doesn't erase issues. If it works, it just puts the ones unfavorable to you somewhat in the background. In a case like this, you may have to draw a person into the sales situation to whom ongoing support is critically important, someone influential enough—clearly a member of the Power Base— to work on your behalf. If you don't, you'll lose. No one has a 100 percent hit rate, and it's better to know that you're in trouble going in, before you waste a lot of time.

There may be other occasions where you'll have to use an indirect strategy to shift a customer's focus from the short term to the long term. In the process, you may have to broaden their perspective on the scope of their needs. Most buying decisions, after all, are made to address immediate require-

93

ments. It takes a while for worn-out wheels to start to squeak, and until they do, they usually don't get any grease. But in some situations, you may be at a disadvantage when it comes to solving a customer's short-term problems. To change the ground rules, you'll have to get their priorities rearranged, so that long-term issues come more to the forefront.

Let's suppose that you are selling for a company that markets automated test equipment (ATE). There is a sales opportunity in your territory in Division A of a rather large company. The division produces a printed circuit board that is used in personal computers. The equipment they are about to buy will give them the ability to test the functional integrity of each board that is built. The vendor you are competing with for this deal is coming in with a direct strategy based on product superiority. Indeed, that vendor's position is strong. For the specific needs of Division A, they probably do have the kind of superiority that will lead to success.

You come into the account, and after working to understand the customer's needs and the organization's Power Base, find that you have nothing on which to base a direct approach of your own. You can't find a source of superiority that would allow you to out-muscle the competition. At this point, you know you need to go the indirect route. All that remains to be defined is how to do so. You begin to fan out in the account. Your first take on the organization's political structure is that the vice-president of Division B is a protégé of the head of Division A. Sensing a potential political interface, you begin to focus on Division B, and any requirements they may have. The people in Division B are designing a new computer work-station, which is only in development. Because, at this stage, there are only a few prototypes being built, their test volume is rather small. But their requirements are much broader and complex than that of Division A's.

The kind of equipment Division A will need performs what is known as "static" testing. Compared to other capabilities, that is a relatively simple function, a "go or no go" test: the board either works, or it doesn't. On the other hand, Division B's needs are more sophisticated. Because they are in a product development mode, they require more dynamic testing abilities. They must be able to determine design faults and, without getting too technical here, diagnose complex problems in the timing of electronic signals, and the like.

At first glance, it would seem that the key here is to create a sales opportunity in Division B. The problem is that the division's needs aren't yet large, pressing, or specific enough to warrant an acquisition of test equipment. They would benefit, however, by having their requirements included in the buying criteria for what Division A is about to purchase. In this case, you want your indirect strategy to build a bridge between Division A and Division B—one that already exists politically—to affect the selection of a vendor. You want the ground rules to shift from A's immediate short-term needs to include . the flexibility to accommodate the needs of Division B. Of course you'll need to construct a business case for standardization and in making the Power Base Principle work, you'll also want to get the head of Division B to make the case to his or her mentor, who happens to be Division A's vice-president, the Fox.

Timed properly—which we'll get into in Chapter 9—the indirect strategy can pull the rug right out from under the competition and, by the way, is a favored approach of the Ivy League street fighter. People from Division B will gradually begin to take a role in the buying decision. At first, your competitor may be pleased by this. At a meeting, someone from Division B may show up, politely asking such questions as, "What you're saying sounds good, but tell me, how would you handle this particular requirement?" At first, your competitor may not perceive the threat, and may write off Division B's input, thinking at most there's another sales opportunity there, somewhere down the line. But later, the picture becomes clearer and the salesperson will begin to feel the ground shifting beneath his or her feet.

Eventually it will become clear that what started with simple, curious questions is becoming an addition to the buying criteria. Instead of being able to close, the best your competitor can do is link to more meetings. He or she may or may not have the product capability to meet the expanded requirements—it really doesn't matter. In either event, the salesperson will have to take time to fully understand the broadened criteria, and then to reconfigure the proposed approach. If you've implemented your strategy well, that opportunity will not exist.

There are many ways to change the ground rules. You can shift the focus away from the product and onto what it does or represents, as we saw in the Cabbage Patch Kids doll example where, all of a sudden, a doll became a companion. You can broaden the application or scope of customer needs, as in the ATE scenario. Or, perhaps, you can even project into the future, making tomorrow's requirements a consideration today. As long as the shift in focus genuinely provides increased value to the customer, you'll be on safe ground, while the competition will be thrown off balance.

There are occasions when you will rule out the direct strategy and also find no satisfactory way to alter the ground rules. When that happens, it's time to consider yet another approach to getting the victory you prize.

Chapter 7

The Divisional Strategy: How to Divide and Conquer the Competition

If the enemy's forces are united, separate them.

—Sun Tzu

A s the name implies, a divisional approach to winning business involves dividing and conquering the competition. It is a cousin of the direct strategy; in fact, someone viewing its application from a tactical perspective probably couldn't tell them apart. But the intent behind the divisional strategy is quite a bit different. You go divisional when you can't bowl the competition over to win the whole pie, but when there's a delicious piece you'd love to sink your teeth into. Your efforts will involve drawing a partition around a select portion of the business, specializing in a particular area. The effect is not so much to displace, or replace, another vendor as it is to complement the market, to add something to it that wasn't there before.

Marketing Applications of the Divisional Strategy

Several years ago, the Miller Brewing Company found themselves in a difficult position. Their share of the beer market was pretty stable, but the market itself wasn't expanding very much. What this meant for Miller was the prospect of a long period of little or no growth, which is usually poison for a corporation's finances. At the time, Miller was approximately in seventh place in the market, miles behind the hands-down industry leader, Anheuser Busch. Management knew they had to do something.

The tendency for companies in these circumstances is to go direct. They beef up advertising budgets and expand their distribution channels. Miller management, however, was a little more savvy. They knew that going head-to-head in a dormant market against the industry leader would be like pushing a large rock up a steep hill. After all, Anheuser Busch was a formidable adversary, with lots of cash and deep, deep pockets. For every distributor Miller pushed, Busch could respond by a factor of ten. A Miller advertising blitz would pale in comparison to the tens of millions of dollars more that Busch had available to devote to counterattack in promotion. Knowing this, Miller's management ruled out a direct onslaught.

The second look through the window of opportunity— through the "indirect" pane—was no more promising for the company. It might have been great fun to try to change the ground rules for the beer drinking public, and try to sell, let's say, the health benefits of drinking beer, in moderation, to reduce stress, assuming such benefits exist. But Miller decided their approach would have to be a bit more conservative, but aggressive nonetheless. They decided on a divisional approach, one aimed at being the first to reach a portion of the market that was, quite literally, untapped. The segment of the population they focused on was the expanding group of people who were concerned about just that—expanding. Miller directed their efforts toward individuals who were diet- and weight-conscious, and who had reduced their intake of beer or foresworn it completely because of its high caloric content.

Thus was born Lite beer. As a result, and with a little help from friends who we'll talk about later, Miller's market share increased dramatically over the next five years, and the company was propelled into the number two spot in the industry. To prove this isn't an isolated application of the divisional strategy, I'll give you another example. If you don't like beer, maybe you like root beer.

Here's how the soft drink business works. Manufacturers—Coca-Cola, Pepsico, and the rest—sell a concentrate to independent bottlers. The bottlers, in turn, add water, carbonate it, and bottle and distribute the final product.

Between the two of them, Pepsi-Cola and Coca-Cola account for over 71 percent of the soft drinks market. Way down at the bottom of the list, with a whopping 2 percent share, is A&W Brands, Inc. Despite their small size, A&W's growth is outpacing all other players, primarily because of heads-up strategic thinking in the corporate offices. A&W has known from the start that they cannot compete directly with the leaders of their industry. For one reason, because of their contract with A&W restaurants, they cannot offer their product to fast-food chains. For another, because of their company's small size and limited market penetration, they cannot expect bottlers to throw over the major manufacturers. What they have done is divide and, if not conquer, impressively prosper. Already having drawn a partition around their efforts by specializing in root beer, the company's approach to bottlers is aimed at achieving the complementary effect the divisional strategy produces. Essentially, the company convinces bottlers that there's always room for a few cases of root beer on their trucks, nestled right in with the Coke and Pepsi, and the bottlers rightfully believe that the products will indeed sell.

Now, the purpose behind a divisional strategy is usually to secure a toehold in a market when just walking right in isn't possible. And, when the toehold is achieved, companies usually like to expand their presence—slowly but surely, one step at a time, never making a lot of noise. That's how they grow, and that's exactly what A&W is doing today. Gradually, the company is expanding its presence. They've successfully introduced a cream soda. They've acquired the grapefruit-flavored soft drink called Squirt, and they've brought out a few new products, as well. But they never have produced—and probably never will—a cola, or a 7UP type of lemon-lime drink. They've done well with the divisional approach, have avoided the big guns, and are understandably determined to stay with what has brought them success.

When most new companies are born, they usually operate in a divisional fashion. The grand strategy for their sales efforts normally represents an effort to serve a portion of the market whose needs are not being fully satisfied by industry leaders. They choose a niche that offers potential profitability, and where they can provide a product or service that would otherwise be unavailable. There are very practical reasons why this is the way businesses evolve, and it produces conditions where virtually everyone benefits. For a start-up business, going head-to-head against large, established competitors is usually an impossible task. By taking a narrow focus and partitioning the market, they get an opportunity to choose an area where they can excel. Customers benefit, too, since the start-up company's entry into the market gives them a wider choice of products, and a stronger likelihood that some vendor will have just the solution to their particular needs.

Even the established vendors get something out of this. Unless the niche marketer represents a direct threat to their main business, industry leaders are freed from the burden of spreading themselves thin and trying to be all things to all people. Of course, if the niche vendor is a threat, or if the business they've created seems lucrative, their success will shine like a beacon and other companies will come at them full force. After all, industry leaders sense an emerging market, and they want it. At that point, conditions have been altered, the profile has changed. The divisional strategy that was so successful may be obsolete, and companies in this position usually have to shift into a direct approach just to stay alive.

An automobile sound system used to be a slapped-in AM radio that was connected to a tinny-sounding speaker on the top of the dash. Then came a network of car stereo shops who would install high fidelity AM/FM stereo/cassette systems along with speakers in your doors. Executives snapped to attention in Detroit. An aftermarket had developed. A radio wasn't a radio anymore, and it wasn't even a sound system. It was a source of incremental revenue. Manufacturers saw the business potential and moved in, using product linking to sell high-margin systems as a dealer option. Suddenly, those local stereo shops found themselves competing with the likes of Chrysler, Ford, and General Motors. Niche vendors who encounter the unwanted attention of such giants have very little in the way of alternatives. Their divisional cover has been blown. They may be swallowed up; they may simply be shoved aside. They may be able to strike a deal. But to survive, and to remain independent, they have to go direct. Whether they will be able to effectively compete is another matter.

Management at Miller knew that the prospect of just such an intense struggle with the beer industry giants was brewing at about the same time they introduced their less-filling/tastes-great product. Help came when they merged with another, much larger resource-rich company to gird for the fight they expected when Busch and others saw the Lite.

Sales Applications of the Divisional Strategy

The principles that apply in general business for the divisional strategy are also true for salespeople at an account level. Whether you work for a small company or an established giant, circumstances will arise from time to time where neither a direct onslaught nor a changing of the ground rules against the competition will work. A number of factors may account for your inability to compete for the whole ball of wax, but it usually comes down either to product capability or to who has the installed base.

On an account level, the divisional strategy is often the best approach when you're trying to penetrate one of the competition's strongholds. Even if you can't meet the needs of some niche in the account, you still may be able to find a way to add on to what one vendor has already installed.

Suppose you work for a company that manufactures communications equipment. An account is about to place an order to upgrade their telephone system, an order so huge that, if you could win it, it would make your year. Your company has very good products, at very good prices, and enjoys an excellent reputation. At first thought, given your assets, you would probably expect to implement a direct strategy, perhaps combining the variations of product superiority and "selling the company." Unfortunately, the customer is very satisfied with the product and service from their existing supplier, a vendor that excels at manufacturing and marketing switching equipment, and specializes at it to the extent that they really don't offer any other products. Your problem is that the customer is going to expand the present system, not replace it. You can't win the business because your product wouldn't be compatible with the installed equipment. In other words, the customer is determined to buy a kind of telephone system that you simply don't have. They're so set on their criteria, from the top of the organization on down, that there will be no opportunity to change the ground rules.

At this point, your ability to see things before they happen becomes critical. Given the size of the pending order, the temptation—and pressure—to fight directly, despite the odds, may be overwhelming. People who yield to this pressure, who knowingly devote untold time and resources to a losing cause, usually do so because they believe there is no alternative. But there is, even when there's no opportunity to change the ground rules. In a situation such as this one where you know, with certainty, that you can't win it all, go out and win whatever piece of the business you can. Maybe, in this case, you can demonstrate value to the customer by installing a voice-mail system if they don't already have one, and the competition doesn't offer it as a product.

Two words characterize what it takes for a divisional strategy to succeed: peaceful coexistence. The product or service you propose must fit in with the customer's overall plans, operations, and installation. If it is inherently incompatible with the existing environment, a divisional strategy will fail. In this case, you would do nothing in your selling efforts to stall the incumbent's progress in winning the order for the expanded telephone service. You would sell the benefits of voice mail as a piggyback on the system, to complement and improve upon it, avoiding at almost all costs any suggestion that adopting your proposal would disrupt the operation in any way. To be sure, you won't get that gigantic order, but you wouldn't have gotten it anyway, not in this case, at least. However, you would get a smaller order, and a small order is preferable to no order at all. With it, you've built a platform to sell from in the future.

The key is to get into the account. Once you're there, you'll provide as much tender loving care to your product as you can, because you'll be nurturing a foundation for future business. Someday, the customer may become dissatisfied with the established supplier of the switching system, and there you are, ready to go into the game. Once you've built credibility in a customer's eyes, and gotten close enough to the Power Base to hear the pinging, opportunities for major orders are bound to come your way. Also, with your foothold in the account, the pressure is on the competition. You have a limited part of the business, but you can focus on it, and dedicate the talents of your best people to its support. The competition has a large installation, and with it, exponentially more pitfalls. The customer is bound to make comparisons between vendors, and every time the competition makes a mistake, they'll be looking over their shoulders. They'll be like aging athletes who know there are hot-handed rookies on the bench. One bad performance in a critical situation, and their jerseys will be hung from the rafters.

Nothing about the divisional strategy should be viewed as being easy. Because this approach is usually aimed at somewhat limited objectives, some people think that partitioning off a piece of business requires less effort and strength than a direct or indirect strategy. In reality, going divisional requires quite a bit of strength; it is simply more narrowly focused. And, because it is essential to work in a quiet and reassuring manner, it can be a very difficult strategy to implement.

With it, you will also need a good measure of political help. Insight about the level of influence of members of the Power Base will be important, and an acute awareness of their agendas and motives will be critical. If you're not careful, your divisional approach will represent more potential political gain for an individual than it will for you to win business. You could become a political yo-yo.

The Sleeper

Anyone who ever played with a yo-yo knows how to make it "sleep." It's the easiest trick in the book. When the string is loosely wound and the yo-yo is thrown with a steady hand, it will just spin on its own at the end of the cord.

At times, an established vendor in an account can become a sleeper. After feeling you own an account for a while, it's pretty easy to get overconfident and let down your guard. In fact, it may get to the point where the customer perceives that your support for them has slipped a bit, and that you're taking the business for granted. Maybe there are problems in the account, not serious ones, but enough minor issues to cause the customer to lose perspective on all the good you've done, and focus only on the difficulties.

Now, imagine a situation like the one described regarding the purchase of communications equipment. You would like to gain access to an account where the customer is about to place a relatively small order for additional equipment, an order that could be a slam dunk for the established vendor. It's not so automatic this time, though, because the incumbent is, or is perceived to be, asleep. You know you probably can't unseat the incumbent, despite their current difficulties, but you do see this small order as a chance to sneak into the account. You find and approach an influential person, who we will call Pete Hastings, for guidance on how to work in the organization. The meeting goes well, and Hastings agrees to champion your cause. With his help, just the right approach, and a little bit of luck, you may be able to steal an order right out from under the incumbent's nose. What you don't know is that Hastings is engaged in an organizational power struggle, and sees an opportunity of his own. He senses a chance to fire off a few good political rounds by capitalizing on the incumbent's difficulties. But his gain may come at your expense.

At this point, what you've done for yourself is much less clear than what you've done for, or to, others. For one thing, you've put the incumbent vendor in a lose-lose situation. For another, you have given Pete Hastings a win-win. What you've done for yourself isn't quite as simple.

Perhaps this order should have been a shoo-in for the incumbent, but with your divisional approach it suddenly becomes a major battle. When Hastings begins to work on your behalf, you start to develop momentum, and receive a lot of attention. About this time, alarm bells go off among the incumbent's supporters. For the established vendor, the seriousness of the situation becomes apparent, and they spring into action. They know their record in the account is the sole cause for this becoming a competitive bid, and they mount a campaign to reclaim their position. They bring in the guns from corporate headquarters. They make high-level commitments to the customer. Their organization renews its support efforts, and begins to take even minor complaints from the customer very seriously. Whether they act effectively and quickly enough will probably determine this buying decision. But remember, the net is a win for Pete Hastings.

If the incumbent's reputation is too far gone to save, you get the order and Hastings wins because he's the guy who brought you in. If the incumbent turns things around and gets the order, Hastings *still* wins, because *he* gets the credit for making them clean up their act. He becomes the corporate hero, the guy who can make vendors straighten up and fly right. Obviously, the incumbent loses if you win the order. But they also lose if they win it themselves. The perception will exist in many minds, probably correctly, that they only got their act together because of the competitive pressure from you, not for the right reasons. Many people in the organization will wonder: if it hadn't been for the prospect of losing an order, what would it have taken to get the vendor off the dime? With a little help and reinforcement from you, they will continue to wonder. They'll always be suspicious that, when things settle down, the incumbent will slip back into the old, negligent pattern. They'll ask: "what will it take to wake up the vendor in the future, when we rely on them even more?" So, even if, in the end, the incumbent gets the order, they've already lost a great deal of credibility. Life will never be the same for them in that account.

For you, a solid chance of winning only exists if you are certain that Pete Hastings' motives are somewhat honorable. Your political value may be exhausted at the instant the incumbent wakes up. At that point, Hastings' objectives are met. He has scored his political victory, and you may be left hung out to dry. A true political bond is an alliance, which is quite a bit different from simply having political support. You never really know for sure where mere "support" is coming from, in terms of motivation. We'll examine that more in Chapter 13.

Walking the Dog

There is an imitation of the divisional strategy commonly known as the puppy dog approach. For some people, it's the only kind of divisional strategy they know how to use. It's a giveaway, a "try it, you'll like it" freebie for the customer. It is intended to get the salesperson's foot in the door, and presumes that, once the product is installed, the customer will become dependent on it and be reluctant to get rid of it. Thus locked in, they would virtually be forced to buy the product.

There are cases where this kind of spin on a divisional approach makes sense, but I think it's often used as a substitute for good selling. It doesn't take a lot of skill to give something away. Ivy League street fighters rightfully believe that their product is worth something.

The presumption behind consigning products at no charge on a trial basis is that the customer assumes no risk. That is usually true. Another presumption is that the salesperson also has nothing to lose. That is often wishful thinking. When your sales strategy essentially puts you in the position of being a benefactor for a customer, you become highly vulnerable from a political point of view. Once again, you become a political yo-yo, and the results you obtain may amount to the exact opposite of what you had hoped for. There's another yo-yo trick called "walking the dog." As before, a skillful political practitioner can use your divisional approach for his or her own ends, and walk your consignment right out of the account when those ends are met.

Let's return to the sales situation we just discussed, but change a few things. As before, you're trying to penetrate the account where the incumbent vendor has fallen asleep at the wheel and a small order is about to be placed. Once again, you approach Pete Hastings to determine whether there is any contribution you can make to his organization. This time, however, he doesn't offer to champion your cause right off the bat. He's more conservative, and is reluctant to take a role. He likes what he hears from you, but he's not entirely convinced. You, however, sense an opening. You propose to install your product on consignment, and to support it at no charge during a trial period. Somewhat to your surprise, Hastings readily agrees. You arrange for delivery, and the equipment is installed shortly thereafter.

How do you feel? If you're like most salespeople, you feel great. After all, how often is a consignment returned? There's a reason it's called the "puppy dog" approach. The customer can't help but commit resources to the product, it becomes a part of their operation, and in time, they begin to rely on it. Of course, the established vendor has an entirely different reaction. For an incumbent, strolling into an account and seeing another vendor's product, especially with an order pending, is like seeing a competitor's name on the sign-in log, only ten times worse. It lights a fire under them, and off they go. Just as before, they will ferociously rededicate themselves to the account, intent on solving all the problems.

There's no better way to wake up a salesperson than to threaten his or her position in the account. In an informal discussion, however, Hastings makes it clear to the incumbent that if they correct the problems and renew their commitment to support, they'll get another chance. As soon as the established vendor takes corrective measures, Pete's objectives are met. The order goes to the incumbent, and much to your surprise, the product you consigned is returned.

A customer is often dependent on vendor support resources. Success can sometimes totally depend on quick access to the vendor's expertise to, let's say, solve a problem with a new installation. So, customers compete for vendor resources and the way they compete is through the vendor's salesperson. Discredit that individual, cause him or her "to lose face," and the customer can find himself or herself in an uphill battle for those precious resources. It all begins when a salesperson's manager and others believe an account is not being well managed, as evidenced by a key loss that gives another company a foothold in the account.

Once again, it's a win-win for Pete. But this time, rather than being a lose-lose for the established vendor, it's very much a win-win for them, too. First, they win the battle against you. Second, the incumbent salesperson becomes a hero. Winning an order is great, but turning around a loss is spectacular. But, all this was done at your expense, as Pete Hastings used you as a vehicle to set up the win-win scenarios.

Call a product giveaway a puppy dog or anything you like, but don't call it a divisional strategy. In fact, don't even call it a sales strategy. A sales strategy, whether it is divisional or one of the other classes, involves *selling* something. Accept no substitutes.

When All Else Fails . . .

If you can't divide and conquer, and if you've already ruled out the direct and indirect strategies as the basis for success, you really only have three options.

First, you could walk away from the opportunity. That doesn't sound very good to most salespeople, and it sounds even worse to sales managers. But there are times you simply shouldn't compete. Part Three of this book will help you determine them, and be convinced you're doing the right thing. A second option is to compete even when you're bound to lose, if for no other reason but to raise the price of victory for the competition. Frankly, unless the investment of your time and resources would be too great, I favor this over unconditional surrender.

Before trying either of the above options, however, you should take one final look through the window of opportunity. Sometimes, the best decision you can get is a "no-decision." The next chapter will tell you about those times when you can slow down a buying process just long enough to gather some strength.

Chapter 8

The Containment Strategy: Using "No-Decision" Tactics to Keep the Competition from Winning

Though the enemy be stronger in numbers, we may prevent him from fighting.
—Sun Tzu

You can use a direct, indirect, or divisional strategy to obtain an order for business. But if you decide that none of these will provide a favorable result, you can implement a containment strategy as a defensive move to keep someone else from succeeding. Just as the divisional strategy is a cousin of the direct approach, differing mainly in intent, the containment strategy is akin to an indirect effort to change the ground rules. With containment, though, you're trying to alter the field of battle in an entirely different way. Rather than trying to change the basis for a buying decision, you'll work to have the decision itself postponed.

In 1812, Napoleon Bonaparte amassed a Grand Armee, an impressive force of 450,000 well-trained troops with an astounding record of military success, and marched on Russia. Perhaps the most competent strategist ever to live, supported by a number of willing (and some unwilling) allies, Napoleon was sure of a victory that would extend his dominion beyond the size of any empire known before. After all, on the surface, the Russians seemed hopelessly outmatched. They lacked the numbers and resources to mount a direct assault as Napoleon progressed. They could hardly change the ground rules—they were, after all, being invaded—and no strategist of Napoleon's caliber would be divided and conquered. For all their deficits, however, the Russians did have one inestimable asset, the harsh and unrelenting ally who became known as "General Winter."

A brilliant strategy can mitigate the effects of tactical blunders, but the best tactics in the world cannot succeed in the face of a fundamentally flawed strategy. Considering how slowly, in those days, a force the size of the Grand Armee moved, and how difficult thousand-mile supply lines were to maintain, Napoleon had launched his campaign dangerously late in the year. Deprived of the resources to aggressively defend their territory, the Russian strategy became one of containment. They would delay Napoleon just long enough, make the Grand Armee's progress just difficult enough, to allow General Winter to tip the scales.

The Russian army met Napoleon's forces not in areas most favorable to victory, but on terrain that would best lead to stalemate. They held their positions as long as possible, and then retreated. As they fled, they burned crops and slaughtered livestock—the foodstuffs that the advancing forces of the time counted on for survival—scorching the earth to deny the invaders nourishment. By the time the French reached their first major objective, Moscow, they were tired, hungry, demoralized, and depleted. The Moscow they captured had already been evacuated and burned, and offered no subsistence. Then came winter, and a long, treacherous retreat with 90 percent casualties for an army defeated by the master strategist's poor strategy, savaged all the way home by nature and a counterattacking Russian army. The French were not beaten on the field of battle in the Russian campaign. They were contained so long that they couldn't win.

In business, market leaders are always vulnerable to erosion. Simply put, there is always a certain amount of dissonance in a customer base—a set of clients who are dissatisfied, another group that is impatient, and so on. A corporation can't be all things to all people, even if some of those people are its most loyal customers. Companies must have a strategy in place for meeting the objective of keeping the customer base that they fought so hard to win.

There are a number of practical reasons why General Motors has a number of divisions. Without doubt, especially for such a gigantic corporation, it makes tangible business sense to have separate operating units, each responsible for its own profit and loss. But there are intangible benefits, as well. You've probably never heard anyone say, "I sure do hate this GM I bought." But there are people who say things such as, "I'll never buy another Pontiac as long as I live!" And you know what? Those people *don't* buy a Pontiac again. Instead, they buy a Chevy. Net-net, General Motors wins. As long as automobiles from various GM divisions maintain separate identities, the corporation contains a good portion of its customer base.

In Chapter 5, I talked about how IBM learned, early in its history, the art of selling the company. At the same time, its salespeople also learned how to contain with the best of them.

The introduction of the FUD Factor (fear, uncertainty, and doubt) to the high-tech industry began as early as the 1940s, when IBM's electronic calculators were often sold largely on the basis of their reliability, in contrast to the more troublesome, albeit more technologically sophisticated, Univac computers. If the horrible prospect of a Univac system crash wasn't enough to sway customers, IBM salespeople pushed hard to get customers to conduct a thorough study before making a final decision. The months that it took to conduct these studies bought time for IBM—it gave their sales teams time to strengthen their political position in the account. At a point in time when technology was quickly developing, this time that IBM bought maximized their chances of improving their product's capabilities during the hiatus.

Decades later, IBM hasn't lost much of its touch when it comes to tying competitors in knots. When such vendors as Digital Equipment or Wang Laboratories introduce advanced products, about all that "Big Blue" has to do is issue a "statement of direction," an announcement of its planned approach. Implicit in the statement is that anything IBM does will become the industry standard, and that customers would be well served to wait until the big dog eats. Many of them do.

In selling, when conditions spell defeat, sometimes the best you can do is hang in there long enough for conditions to change. You need to formulate a containment strategy of your own.

How to Contain

Suppose you're competing in a situation where a customer plans to make a buying decision in ninety days for a particular kind of product. The problem is that while your company plans to offer such a product, it won't be announced for some time. Plus, the customer is the skeptical kind—any attempt to sell "futures" just won't work. What you need is time, an extra ninety days added to the evaluation and decision process. You know you can't (and shouldn't) get a delay if it adversely affects the customer, but as this sales situation peaks, it becomes clear that you have to contain the situation long enough for your product to be formally introduced, so the customer will know it's real.

One approach would be to start bringing new people into the account. You'll want whomever you can think of—as long as they have something genuinely of value to contribute—whether they are from marketing, research and development (R&D), or wherever, to become active. You may even be able to bring in a consultant, perhaps to do a study. One effect of this approach will be to get more of the customer's people involved, too, which always slows things down. The people you bring in will search for new and pertinent issues; the net result you're looking for will be that the customer has a real incentive to move at a somewhat more ponderous pace toward a decision.

When a sales situation is peaking, a short-term containment approach may involve taking the customer off-site. In many cases, the added value of taking a prospect to a reference account where you have a successful installed base is that it gives the prospect, when he or she becomes a customer, people to network with in the future. It's very possible that a customer will genuinely benefit from being introduced to others who are trying to solve similar problems. When this happens toward the conclusion of a sales cycle, the containment you're looking for becomes a by-product.

A visit to your corporate headquarters may also be beneficial. If you do plan such a visit well, you'll want to select a good mix of people to take to headquarters, such as a pairing up of the customer's executives with your executives, their wizards with yours. You may want to do all this on a non-disclosure basis, so that you or your management can discuss what your company has in the works—in a tactical statement of direction—to convince the customer that you're not just blowing smoke. The timing of such a corporate visit properly is also extremely important, especially if you sense you're in real trouble. When you're losing, you usually have a great deal of difficulty contacting people and getting information. As much as salespeople don't like getting bad news, customers don't particularly enjoy giving it. So, when an order is about to go to another vendor, you're often very much in the dark, just at the time when you most need solid data. But, when you have the customer cloistered on your turf, you have intense exposure to key people at that very critical time. You can learn an awful lot, which is why it's difficult to understand why some salespeople don't accompany their customers on such a trip. Without your presence, the whole purpose of the visit, from a sales point of view, is defeated.

You can go to any reasonable ends to implement a containment strategy, and at times those ends may actually include introducing another competitor into the process. This sounds bizarre, but if you're not going to win, sometimes it makes sense to have some control over who you lose to. Suppose you're working in an account—we'll call you Vendor A—and it's pretty clear you are about to lose to Vendor B, who is running an out-and-out direct strategy based on product superiority. Although your product can also essentially do the job for the customer, B's product is somewhat more advanced in its major functionality. To catch up, your product needs major enhancements, which are a bit down the road. What's worse is that Vendor B's product has a key feature that your product lacks, a capability that is so critically important to the customer that a change of the ground rules is out of the question. In fact, even after your product is improved, it still will not possess this key feature. All in all, your take on the situation is that you're not going to win.

Losing an order here and now is going to be bad enough, but what's worse about this particular defeat is that it will lead to more setbacks in the future. Once installed in this account, Vendor B will be able to product link until the cows come home. Every time the customer wants to expand the installation, the order for additional equipment will most likely go to Vendor B, all because of that one key feature you cannot offer. Although a defeat seems inevitable, it may be possible to avoid a total loss. Suppose you know of a certain Vendor—Vendor C— who is a small niche marketer of an excellent product. Their equipment does not compete with yours or with Vendor B's for major installations because its scope is limited, but their product does one thing well—better than anyone's, in fact— it peacefully coexists with major products such as the ones you and Vendor B represent. That one task Vendor C performs so well happens to be the critical function that is so central to the customer's requirements.

An advantage of having Vendor C involved is that their line of offerings is too narrow to allow them to product link in the future. And you don't have to do anything questionable to introduce them into the sales situation. You can frankly suggest to the customer that, given the significance of that special feature, they would be wise to look at what Vendor C has to offer. In the process, you'll get credit for having a genuine interest in the customer's needs. That may not be enough to overcome your problems—Vendor B still may be so superior that they get the order—but the niche player's presence takes away Vendor B's ability to lock up the future business.

Remember that your product's development is going to catch up with Vendor B's one of these days, and by the time future orders roll around in the account, your product should at least be at parity with theirs on the major capabilities. You'll still lack that one special feature, but if Vendor C is taking care of it, who cares? By introducing Vendor C, even if you lose the short-term order, you will have contained Vendor B's penetration in the account.

When to Contain

When a containment strategy has succeeded, and caused a decision to be delayed, you can next decide which of the other classes of strategy will get you an order. Now that you're off the defensive and back in the game, you can choose a direct, indirect, or divisional approach to win business. Just remember that with a successful containment strategy, no one is going to win an order for a while—including you. And *before considering containment*, be sure that none of the other classes of strategy can work for you. The last thing in the world you want to do is accidently contain yourself.

In 1981, Adam Osborne revolutionized the still young personal computer business by introducing a low-cost, portable machine with bundled software. Naturally, a host of competitors followed suit. Unfortunately for Osborne, his company reached a critical point in any start-up's growth just when a shakeout was beginning in the computer industry. For venture capitalists, giddy optimism about high technology was turning into a more balanced caution just when Osborne needed cash, and it was a struggle for the company to secure financing. Earnings went in the wrong direction at the worst possible time, right before the company's initial public stock offering, which had to be delayed. To compound matters, dealers cut back on Osborne orders because of their dissatisfaction with service. But what killed Osborne Computer Corporation, more than any of these factors, was a self-inflicted containment strategy it inadvertently ran against itself.

Although the company's profits had been shaky, sales of the Osborne 1 were reasonably healthy. They might very well have remained so, had not Osborne announced, in early 1983, that it would bring out a new model of its computer. The problem was that the new computer wasn't ready, and wouldn't be for some time. For established companies, such premature announcements can be embarrassing, but for a one-product company, it spells disaster. When you tantalize customers by suggesting that if they think they like today's product, just wait until tomorrow's comes out, customers will do just that. They'll wait. Especially the most loyal ones, because they get as excited about the new product as you are. That's what became of Osborne Computer Corporation. At the height of its vulnerability, customers waited, orders dissipated, and cash flow evaporated. Osborne contained itself. Deprived of funds to nourish and sustain it, not to mention to complete development of the new product, the company disappeared. In a sales situation, keep a careful watch on your enthusiasm. Make sure that the people you bring into the account keep their focus—and the customer's—on today's issues and solutions.

As with the other classes of strategy, certain conditions must exist for a containment approach to succeed, and even to be reasonably considered. First, the customer must perceive value in postponing the decision. A clever but worthless delaying tactic will only serve to annoy the customer and damage your credibility. You'll lose the right to a fair hearing in the future. Second, the amount of time you need to delay must be reasonable. When there are real issues driving a buying decision, a containment strategy will generally work for a period of weeks—perhaps a few months—but no longer. Quite frankly, if the decision could be delayed as long as a year or more, you probably don't have a well-qualified opportunity to begin with. Finally, there must be a strong likelihood that you can truly meet the customer's needs after the postponement. If that new product of yours isn't on the horizon, and never will be, you're wasting your time trying to contain the decision, and you're certainly not doing the customer any favors. From a competitive point of view, you would be better served by choosing a different class of strategy. Who knows? Maybe you would get lucky and win. At the very least, you would make life more difficult for the competition.

Although a containment strategy is a defensive approach to a sales objective, one aimed at producing a "no-decision" instead of an order, it can be a potent weapon in your arsenal. At the heart of every Ivy League street fighter is the determination not only to win, but to prevent the competition from winning. A well thought-out and executed strategy gives you the ability to exercise a certain amount of control over the sales outcome and the timing of the decision. Having control is a function of setting the pace for the competition.

But strategy is not created in a vacuum. Each sales situation you encounter is unique. The competitive threat varies. Even if you have a favorite class of strategy, the skill in Ivy League street fighting rests in being versatile enough to be able to employ them all, to use the right one at the right time, and to execute it effectively. That is the difference between a sales strategy and a *competitive* sales strategy.

Chapter 9

Setting a Competitive
Sales Strategy

The opportunity of defeating the enemy is
provided by the enemy himself.

—Sun Tzu

Through your window of opportunity, you can see much more than just your sales target and the best way to approach it. Off in the distance, the competition is closing in on horseback, kicking up a cloud of dust. A strategic vision not only streamlines your efforts; it helps you determine where, when, and how to knock the bad guys out of the saddle.

Let's put you into a difficult, competitive selling environment where all of your strategic skills will be called upon to produce a victory. (All the companies and individuals mentioned here, by the way, are completely fictitious.) You work for a computer company, and are competing against two other vendors for an order in the Amalgamated Services Corporation, a conservative, rather old-fashioned company. Their industry, however, has become increasingly competitive. Foreign and domestic firms alike are challenging them in a way they've never experienced. As a result, there is a concerted effort afoot in the the company to revitalize and realign themselves to deal with a more intense competitive climate. Nevertheless, those championing this cause have encountered some rather stiff internal resistance. However, with the twenty-first century fast approaching, the company has at last decided to bring their operations into the twentieth, and take advantage of technological advances. Right now, there is a heavy manual paper flow from the point where salespeople take an order, to the order being processed, and then on to inventory control and shipping.

At an industry trade show, Bob Evans, the company's vice-president of operations, learned how this kind of process could be automated. When he returned, he began to build momentum for an automation project in Amalgamated. He saw some benefits for his own department, and even greater ones for other divisions. (Evans is a fast-moving star in the organization who has done this kind of thing before, even when it didn't have direct impact on his own area.) He built up a base of support for the idea, and though it took some convincing, the entire executive staff finally coaxed Ellen Murphy, the CFO, through whom every major decision must pass, to free up funds and acquire a system.

Amalgamated doesn't have a management information systems (MIS) department, given that only their accounting and payroll systems have been automated. Instead, they have a data center that falls under the finance department's purview, supervised by Henry Walker, who, on the side, advises various departments on how to automate such tasks as financial forecasting and word processing with stand-alone or clustered personal computers.

Walker works for Ellen Murphy who, three years ago, drove the decision to automate accounting and payroll. Murphy is happy with the systems that were installed and with the vendor who installed them. She wants to be sure that whomever is selected for the large automation project provides service and support on the same level she's getting now. So, although she has given Henry Walker the responsibility for selecting a vendor for the automation project—because he is the most knowledgeable person in the company about computers—she has reserved the right to have the final say in approving the selection.

To round out the profile:

- The order at stake is worth $1.3 million.
- Amalgamated will definitely, irreversibly, buy the entire system from only one vendor. Take my word for it.
- They will definitely make a final decision and place an order in four weeks. Trust me on this.

That's what you see of the sales terrain. Your company, by the way, is only about two years old. Its founder was once a senior executive at an established vendor in your industry. In part, he made the move because his entrepreneurial spirit was being stifled in a large corporation. More compelling was his dissatisfaction with the company's stodginess when it came to keeping up on technology. Your company was formed with a key part of its mission being to offer only the most state-of-the-art products possible, and you do.

You've actually entered this sales situation rather late. About all you've been able to do so far is gather information. Naturally, you've talked about your company and your product, but mostly you've asked questions, trying to get the lay of the land. Your initial impressions are not very encouraging. The first vendor you're competing with is Comcorp, which is, coincidentally, the firm your company's founder left.

Although Comcorp is no technological giant, they do have solid workhorse products. And while their technology isn't quite state-of-the-art, they have a wide enough product line to allow them to configure a sound, safe approach to meeting Amalgamated's broader needs. The financial tracking system already installed in Amalgamated is theirs. As you might expect, Ellen Murphy favors them, and has made this exceedingly clear to Henry Walker. The importance of Ellen Murphy's desires are not insignificant for Henry Walker. Not only does he work for her, he knows that with the new computer system, Amalgamated will need to create a real MIS department at some point. Someone will have to be its manager, and Henry would like the job. He doesn't consider himself a shoo-in for it, but he knows that the work he does in the selection process, which is his first real crack at doing something significant in the company, will go a long way toward determining whether Murphy gives him the nod.

The second vendor in this deal is Quadtex. Like Comcorp, they have a wide range of well-established products, but they also have a new line that incorporates many technological advances. For the past several months, they've been aggressively working to build market share with the new products, and have been actively converting their existing customer base to them. Because of this emphasis, Quadtex's first approach to Amalgamated was to sell the new technology. They met several times with Henry Walker, and even a few times with Ellen Murphy, to tell their product's story. Unfortunately for them, they didn't get anywhere, even though Walker was very interested in learning about the new technology, and seemed to be leaning in the direction of a high-tech approach to Amalgamated's needs. But Quadtex's efforts stalled as Ellen Murphy made it plain that their product was too sophisticated, and not well enough established in the field. As a result, Quadtex's proposals now reflect their older technology, which is very similar in features and price to Comcorp's product.

Sharpening Your Vision

Just as the good general develops a perception of the face of the country, you now understand the ground on which you'll be competing. In every sales situation, the more accurate a profile you have of the conditions and circumstances that victory will require, the better chance you have of formulating a winning strategy. Given the terrain, the question becomes: who holds the high ground? Based on the field of battle as it is defined, which vendor would win if the decision were to be made right now? If your analysis of the ground rules shows that the competition is ahead, you can expect them to engage in a direct strategy. From whatever source that is strongest, whether it is product, reputation, or installed base, they will attempt to seize the initiative and drive toward an order. From this foundation, you will formulate your strategy. Extending Sun Tzu's wisdom, the key to victory lies not in defeating the competition, but in defeating the competition's *strategy*. The strategy contains their strength, but no matter how strong they are, it also contains the vulnerability you will attack.

Clearly, Comcorp is the primary threat in this sales campaign. Equally obvious is that their strategy is a direct one. By the strength of their product's reliable performance, coupled with a solid company reputation, they will capitalize on their existing position in Amalgamated to proceed directly from opportunity to order. So, here's my question of you: how are you going to win this business? By the way, you can (and will) win this deal. I know there is some information that is sorely lacking. You have an advanced product, but I haven't described any of its capabilities, and I haven't told you anything about your pricing. Frankly, I could have told you even less about this situation, and you could still devise a winning strategy. You just go to the window and take a few minutes to think about which class of strategy would best give you a chance to win this deal. Choose one. If you want to go even further, grab a piece of paper and write down a one-sentence strategy statement that characterizes the nature of the sales campaign you would wage.

Direct versus Direct

Your first alternative is to try to match Comcorp's strategy with a direct approach of your own. You could go in and enthusiastically demonstrate that your product is the best there is. You could even try to capitalize on the fact that your company's founder left Comcorp, intent on outshining them in the industry; however, you'd get exactly the same results Quadtex got with a similar attempt: none. In fact, Quadtex's failed effort in just that vein pushed them so far back that their strategy today is a mirror-image "me-too" version of Comcorp's. Before using a direct strategy in this, or in any, situation, ask yourself two questions:

- Do I have a *clearly* superior position?
- If so, can I sustain it?

For centuries, military strategists applied a simple formula to determine the potential success of a direct assault on opposing forces. The test was whether they had three-to-one superiority over the enemy, whether in troop strength, firepower, or the aggregate. The principle was handed down from times when one relatively well-protected defender on a hill could hold off two attackers. Even with large forces, without three-to-one superiority, field commanders ruled out a direct assault. With the continuing evolution of modern weaponry, the three-to-one rule has, to an extent, gone by the boards in military engagement. But it's not a bad maxim for salespeople to live by in competitive engagement. You may not be able to quantify a threefold edge, but you should be somewhat certain that you have an overwhelming, compelling advantage before relying on a direct approach. And even when you do have a clear superiority, whether you can sustain it is always open to question, and should be examined carefully. It's important to have strength at the beginning of a sales campaign, but it's even more critical to have it at the closing. If your superiority tapers off midway through, you're dead. Before going direct, always put yourself in your competitor's shoes and ask, "If I were in their place, how would I defeat my own strategy?"

If the competition has some base of support in the account, even a minor one, watch for their attempt to change the ground rules. If they have no presence, expect them to try to partition off some piece of the business, reducing the field of battle. If they are strong, but unable to effectively compete, expect an effort to contain your progress. Every move you anticipate will give you an opportunity to preempt competitive maneuvers, shore up your defenses, and sustain your advantage.

To Divide? To Contain?

In Amalgamated, sustaining superiority is a moot point, because you don't have any superiority to begin with. You have a sophisticated product in terms of technology, but one look through the window of this sales opportunity shows that your product's superiority doesn't produce any *competitive* superiority. There may be other accounts where it would put you into the lead, but not here.

We can take quick glances through the window and rule out two other classes of strategy, as well. The divisional strategy is out, because the customer is bound and determined to buy one system from one vendor for one set of needs. For whatever reason, their decision in this regard is immutable.

A containment strategy, on the other hand, may seem attractive, given that you've entered the sales situation rather late. But remember that any time you consider containment, and well before you think about what issues you would introduce to slow down the sales cycle, you should dig a bit deeper in the account. Determine why the customer intends to make a decision in the stated time frame, which in our hypothetical account is four weeks. Your examination of Amalgamated will reveal that they are financing the acquisition with a low-interest bank lending commitment that will expire in—you guessed it—four weeks. It's a "use it or lose it" situation. They won't draw on the funds until a good decision is made, but they're not about to lose them just to give you a bit more selling time. So containment, too, is out.

Very quickly, very simply, you've come to a decision that for many people is long and arduous—you've defined the exact nature of the sales campaign you must wage to win this account. By process of elimination, you know your strategy must be indirect. You can't divide, you can't contain, and the ground rules don't favor you. Therefore, the ground rules must be changed. At this point, you don't know exactly *what* you'll do, but you do know what the *results* of all your efforts must be. By whatever means—whatever tactics you employ—you must effect a shift in the customers' buying criteria.

They must put aside their desire for the safe, standard, old reliable well-established product lines and shift into the fast lane of newer high technology. But keep in mind the two conditions that must exist for an indirect strategy to succeed: your timing must be right, and you must be working with the right people.

Timing

In this situation, because you'll be using an indirect strategy, your late entry to the account can actually work to your advantage. Even if you had been working with Amalgamated for several months, you wouldn't want to introduce a change in the ground rules until very late in the sales cycle. The intended effect of an indirect strategy is to pull the rug out from under the competition, to use their strength and size against them. In Amalgamated, there's no point in tripping up Comcorp if they have time to get up, dust themselves off, and trounce you. The indirect approach has something in common with comedy: timing is everything. I've seen situations, some with very long sales cycles, where a street-wise competitor determined rather early that a change in the ground rules would be necessary to win business, but wisely held back for quite some time. In those circumstances, because you're present in the account, you may actually have to appear to go direct (perhaps with a rather weak direct approach, at that) until the time when introducing the change in the ground rules is most favorable.

Holding your fire until just the right moment is absolutely mandatory and takes a lot of discipline. It may also require that you put your ego in your back pocket. When you've come up with a winning solution to the customer's needs *and* to defeating your competition, it may be hard to keep your enthusiasm in check. But you must. If the length of the sales cycle is not clearly defined, err on the late side of working to change the rules. Waiting too long may make things harder for you, but acting too soon will completely negate the effects of an indirect approach.

The Right People

To win Amalgamated, you're going to have to upset Comcorp's apple cart. But you cannot push it over by yourself; you need help. When it comes right down to it, *you* can't change the ground rules for a buying decision at all—only the customer can. You can work to induce a shift, but for it to occur, you must give the right person the right reasons. It takes some clout to alter buying criteria, and the lower a sales contact is in the organization, the more unlikely it is that he or she can do so. In Amalgamated, Henry Walker either can't or won't change the rules that currently prevent you from winning. So to whom can you turn? Who has a significant amount of power in this organization, has a vested interest in the decision, and may have reason to support you? To help you out, I've illustrated the pertinent organization chart for Amalgamated in Figure 9.1, including the Fox and the Power Base.

Selling is a lot like detective work. They have suspects, we have prospects. They find accomplices, we find allies. They close in on perpetrators, our version is buyers. Detectives also know they must have three things to get what they want (a conviction): opportunity, means, and motive. They must be able to prove that the accused could have committed the crime, was capable of it, and had reason to do so.

132

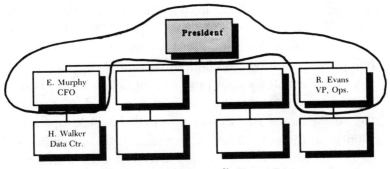

Figure 9.1. Amalgamated's Power Base.

Don't be disturbed if you considered Bob Evans to be a Fox, based on what I told you about him. He's not, but only because the president is so very powerful. Evans, however, like Ellen Murphy, is clearly influential. In this case, you would make no mistake by somewhat overestimating Evans' influence, because you need him very much. He has the opportunity to change the ground rules—four weeks remain before the final decision will be made. He has the means: he's the vice-president of operations, is affected by the decision, has influence in the organization, and originated the idea to automate.

It's up to you to provide the motive. Suppose you approach Evans on the basis that you're trying to better understand Amalgamated's business so you can propose the most insightful solution to their needs. Given that the decision to automate was originally his, ask him how he would suggest you frame your efforts within the context of what's most important to Amalgamated's corporate direction? During your discussion with Evans, you grant that the current buying criteria will produce a solution to Amalgamated's immediate needs. But, drawing on what you learn from his description of what compelled him to propose automation, you begin to push some of his hot buttons. You describe how even more could be done to improve operations by ambitiously capitalizing on technology. You discuss how your product uniquely provides better, beneficial functionality at a higher rate of speed. You suggest that Amalgamated's needs will grow to make these capabilities essential in the not-too-distant future, and that flexibility will become critical—flexibility only achieved with a high-technology decision today. This is no mere product pitch—everything you say is directly based on the company's challenges as Evans presented them.

At this point, if Bob Evans is tempted to reassert a voice in the automation project, you must remember two critical lessons from Chapter 3. Considerations must occur to you that may not occur to someone like Bob right away. First, there is inherent risk in working with a relatively new vendor on an important project. Second, if Evans works to change the ground rules for a project that Ellen Murphy has been charged with, he will assume personal, political risk. Evans may recognize these risks from the start but even if he doesn't, they'll dawn on him eventually. You, however, must be aware of them going in, and begin working to minimize Bob's risk right away. As you recall, you drive down risk by driving up value. You must demonstrate that you, and your company, are competent to make the project succeed. You must send out strong signals—pings—to indicate that you're savvy to the political considerations, and that you'll take your direction from Bob. Once Evans is convinced that the risks involved in siding with you are manageable, and far outweighed by the benefits of working with you, he has the motive to act: value. He will take the opportunity, and use whatever means are available to him.

Important political factors will come into play in a situation like the one I've described, but we'll examine them in detail in Chapter 11. For now, I want to return to the indirect strategy you've employed in this account. There's much more fun ahead before this order is signed. Let's move ahead a few weeks in time. Days before the decision was to be finalized, the ground rules were changed. Instead of an established, conventional product, Amalgamated will purchase a high-technology solution to their present and future needs.

Closing In

The rug has been pulled out from under Comcorp. Their erstwhile superiority has vanished. Like Samson, their strength has been clipped away, and they are helplessly chained to the pillars of the temple. Unlike Samson, they won't regain the strength to bring down the roof. It's too late.

Remember Quadtex? They spent most of the sales campaign in Comcorp's shadow, meekly reminding the customer "we can do that, too." When your indirect strategy knocked Comcorp out of the box, guess what happened to Quadtex? You may have gotten the proverbial two birds with one stone—or did you? Quadtex has a high-technology product, too. They tried to sell it very early in the sales campaign, and were rebuffed. But now, the game has changed. If you were in their shoes, what would you do?

Nothing predicts future behavior better than past behavior. For months, Quadtex has been running a "me, too" sales campaign. The odds are, they'll do it again. As a result, your indirect strategy hasn't brought you that much closer to victory; it's only gotten Comcorp out of your hair. That may have been fun, but being neck and neck in a two-horse race days before a final decision isn't much to crow about. Fortunately, this hasn't happened yet. We'll pick up this story toward the end of Chapter 10. Some salespeople would hope that Quadtex would simply give up. Most would idly hope that the customer will grow tired of the Quadtex salesperson's "me, too's." An Ivy Leaguer would make sure of it, using street-fighting tactics.

Chapter 10

Street Fighting Tactics for Keeping Competitors at Bay

The highest form of generalship is to balk the enemy's plans.

—Sun Tzu

When making a long, difficult ascent, good mountain climbers look back almost as often, and as far, as they look ahead. When they see conditions on the upper mountain turning bad, a principle kicks in: "When in doubt, chicken out." Safety lies in only one direction—down. But descending a mountain quickly is also fraught with peril. At that critical moment, you either know how to get down safely or you don't. Your risk is very high if you have to figure out the way while you descend.

In any sales situation, the closer you come to winning, the closer you come to losing. It is at that point, when the sales cycle peaks, that there is precious little room for error. It is then that the full force of a competitor's countermeasures will be felt. There's no time for analysis and planning, only execution. Assertiveness is important, but preparation is critical.

When all is said and done, managing a peaking sales situation is an exercise in being strategically proactive.

Loss Recovery

When generals devise a plan of battle, they must include one critical provision before the campaign can be launched: a procedure for retreat. Generals know that in the heat of battle, particularly when things are going wrong, there is no time to plan. If a plan doesn't already exist, there's a very poor chance of getting the army out of trouble intact.

To achieve maximum control in a sales campaign, you must take steps to mitigate the effects of potential difficulties. No matter how tactically proficient you are at overcoming obstacles, some problems cannot be dealt with on the fly. Indeed, many times, you don't even know how serious a problem you have until it's too late. When there's something significant on the line in a highly charged environment, your sensors tend not to be very accurate. There's too much emotion involved, and the positive attitude all salespeople need to maintain can cause them to block out negative vibrations. A philosopher once said that an optimist is someone who doesn't have much experience. I would say that an optimist is someone who hasn't seen a major deal go south in the eleventh hour of a sales campaign. When you sense you're in trouble, what you often have on your hands is a disaster. While your instruments merely suggest that engine number one is sputtering a bit, in reality, your wings are on fire.

A loss recovery plan is the selling version of the general's provision for retreat. It will answer the important question; "If I sense I'm losing, what will I do, and who will I do it with?" It is best prepared early in the sales campaign. You put it in a drawer, and if you're lucky, you'll never have to take it out. But if you must, it will give you a much better chance of doing the right things at that critical moment when you smell smoke.

Getting the Facts

It all begins when you sense that you're slipping. Customers don't return calls, you experience a certain distance in the relationship just when it should be getting tighter and stronger. At that unfortunate time when you sense the order falling away, the first thing you'll need is a meeting with the Fox. If possible, you'll want the meeting to occur within twenty-four hours. The sooner, the better. Now, put yourself in the shoes of that Fox. He's either making the decision or he's driving the selection process from behind the scenes, which has included a number of vendors, and has gone on for several months. Over time, the choice has been narrowed to two possible suppliers. Now, the evaluation is complete, a preliminary decision made, and it is about to be finalized.

The losing salesperson—from Vendor B—has gotten wind of the decision and has called the Fox, asking quite frankly (and properly), whether he would choose Vendor B if the decision were to be made today. The Fox knows he's being trial-closed, and though it makes him uncomfortable, out of fairness he's going to feel compelled to give an honest answer. He tells the salesperson the bad news, who asks if he can meet with the Fox the next day to discuss the situation, giving the right reasons—wanting to understand what happened,

139

wanting insight to be better prepared for the future, wanting the relationship to continue—all the normal stuff.

Do you think the Fox would want to meet with this salesperson the next day? The odds are that the answer is "no." The Fox knows that the salesperson knows a defeat is imminent, and wants to try to turn the situation around. But the Fox really doesn't want to start the day with a salesperson twisting his arm, so he resists the suggestion. And even though he may not give a flat "no," that meeting is *not* going to take place in the near future—not soon enough for it to do any good for the salesperson—if the Fox can help it. For the salesperson to ask for a meeting at this juncture is much less likely to bring about results than to request one early in the sales campaign. And, a formal appeal for such a meeting isn't going to be nearly as powerful as an informal one.

In a winning sales campaign most of the elements of a loss recovery plan will never be implemented, but one of them should be—and as early in the process as possible. Suggest to the customer that, should you win the order, that it would help you to have a meeting immediately after a decision is made. Explain how the insights you gain will assist you in planning implementation, and make sure that you do the best possible job for the customer. Add that even in the event you don't get the order, you would still appreciate the meeting as a professional courtesy and as a personal favor, so that you'll have the kind of understanding that will allow you to do a better job in the future. If possible, estimate the length of the sales cycle and gain agreement to at least a general time frame for the meeting. This way, the request is more a reminder and less an appeal; it also has the added impetus of being informal and personal in nature.

Getting the Truth

In the meeting itself, there are two things you'll need to do. One is obvious: you'll have to develop an accurate understanding of the issues. You'll need to find out why you're losing. The objections that you discover, which at this stage tend to have a certain ring of finality, are the issues that must be resolved if you are going to have any chance of recovering a losing situation. Objections are always more revealing than, in general, salespeople know them to be. Motivational speakers like to say that every objection is really an opportunity. As a homily, it can't be beat. But it's more true from a strategic perspective than many of those lecturers will ever know. Objections always reveal tangible problems, but at the same time, if you're looking at them in depth and asking the right questions, they reveal a lot more. For one thing, they tell you about the competition's strategy. In particular, when a vendor is using a direct strategy, issues they've successfully advanced take hold in the customer's criteria. They are placed in a register, a mental table that compares that vendor's product features to yours. The manifestations of those issues are objections, and by finding a thread among them you can accurately calibrate the essence of the competition's direct approach, whether it is of the product superiority, selling the company, or product-linking variety. Even a lack of objections, to a degree, unmasks the competition's strategy. If they're being so quiet that they haven't placed their issues foremost in the customer's considerations, I would be inclined to suspect a divisional approach, or the presence of an intentionally weak direct strategy that cloaks what will become a late-inning, indirect attempt to change the ground rules.

Digging deeper, there is even more to be learned from a buyer's objection. We're all trained to ask why something is important to a customer, but there's a question that is even more important to the success of an Ivy League sales campaign: *to whom* is it important?

The hidden opportunity in every objection is to test the degree to which you have successfully aligned yourself politically in an account. Figure 10.1 shows a snapshot of the Power Base of an organization. (First names only are used to keep it simple.)

Let's say that Barney is the decision maker in your sales campaign. He has stated a number of reasons why he's not inclined to go with your approach. Directly, or indirectly, it becomes clear to you that these are genuine issues, that Barney really does have the power to decide, and that the objections are coming from his view of the situation. Happily, you can deal with all of his concerns, very much to his satisfaction,

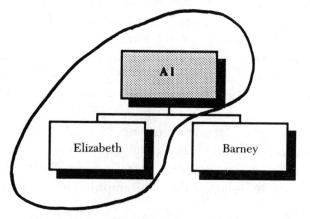

Figure 10.1. The political source of objections.

and put your sales effort back on track. That's good news. It would have been safer to deal with these problems early in the cycle, but even if it's late, as long as other factors cooperate, you might be all right.

Now, let's change the situation. Barney isn't involved. Elizabeth is the decision maker, and she is the true source of the objections. Again, you successfully deal with the concerns, so again, you stave off disaster. Not bad.

That was simple, so let's complicate it a bit. Let's let Elizabeth be the decision maker again, but this time, when she tells you why she's leaning toward your rival, you hear pinging. It begins when you ask for clarification on the significance of the issues Elizabeth has brought up. As she explains, you gain valuable insight that you wish you had possessed earlier, and the pinging gets louder. So, you go a step further. You turn up your sonar full blast. You ask Elizabeth; "Who in the organization are these issues most important to?" And, by both statement and inference, you learn that the objections really come from Al's take on the organization's requirements. Elizabeth is calling the signals, but the plays are being sent in from the bench by Al. Fortunately, as long as you can formulate an effective response that will satisfy Elizabeth, you probably still will be okay. It would be far different if it were Barney who had the ball. Elizabeth is in the Power Base. Elizabeth, because of the value she contributes and for which she is recognized, has credibility in Al's eyes. Al can rely on her to get done what he wants done. She can go back to Al and report that all the issues with you have been resolved and that she's satisfied you can do the job.

With Barney, it's another story. Barney isn't in the Power Base. For whatever reason, he hasn't been able to work his way into the inner sanctum of influence. If Al is really calling the shots, Barney has no discretion when it comes to execution. His is not to reason why. Influence only flows out of a Power Base. On the formal level, you could resolve all the issues with Barney, but it wouldn't do you any good. Unlike Elizabeth, Barney can't simply go back to Al and say "it's all set," and he probably wouldn't even try. He hasn't the credibility. If you've ever successfully dealt with objections—or so you thought—only to find them come up again and again, you've encountered a Barney and Al situation. You were doing all the right things, but there was a disconnect when it came to getting them to the right people. Because you lacked political alignment (and because the competition probably had it), the recurring objections became, for your sales efforts, the death of a thousand cuts.

You would be safest in any of the versions of the story we've been discussing if earlier you had gained direct access to the Fox. You had it indirectly when Al's concern was expressed by Elizabeth, and when Elizabeth had the power and credibility to resolve it. Had you enjoyed direct access to Al, the problem may never have come up at all, which is particularly important when you're dealing with someone like Barney.

When it is known in an organization that the Fox is comfortable with you, the concerns other people may have become neutralized. Such is the power of a Fox. Barney, for example, isn't about to push his concerns at the expense of his position in the company. That's what direct access to Al does for you. Without a clear path to the Fox, or at least indirect access through a member of the Power Base, you'll only be able to address objections that come to the surface. Unfortunately, not all do, especially when Foxes are involved. They work so quietly, and are so well respected, that their concerns often never are explicitly stated. They don't have to be. In an organization, people know when a Fox has a problem with, or a bias against, a particular vendor. They may not know the nature of the problem, but it really doesn't matter. They won't act in a manner that is contrary to what they perceive the Fox desires. If the Fox has a problem with you, and you lack insight to the Power Base and alignment with its members, you may never know specifically what the issues are. But you won't make headway with anyone, anywhere.

No matter how good you are at handling objections, you won't be able to overcome the most dangerous ones—objections that originate in the Power Base—unless you have political alignment. Without it, even if the Fox's objections surface, no response of yours will prevent them from recurring. More likely, they won't surface, and you can't fight what you can't see.

Securing a Commitment

Given the ability and opportunity to get to the right people, a key part of preparing a loss recovery plan is the installation of an *escape vehicle*, something that will get you off the mountain and out of danger. An escape vehicle is a mechanism that will allow someone to reverse a decision without damaging his or her credibility. We'll examine it in detail a bit later. Turning around a sales situation that is slipping away isn't easy, but some competitors leave the door wide open for you to do exactly that. Because they don't secure their position when things are going well, they invite their own demise.

Three conditions must exist in order to bring a sales cycle to a close. The customer must be ready, willing, and able to make a decision. That means the customer must have reviewed all the information; be willing, in that management supports his or her making a decision, and be able, in that the necessary

145

funding is present. If any one of those three states are missing, an attempt to close will be premature, and will not be successful.

On the surface, the closing process is simple. To begin, you simply ask for the order, politely but directly. Then, you keep your mouth shut. Few things are more disconcerting to a customer who is ready, willing, and able to decide than a salesperson who talks past the close. At this stage, you will get either a "yes" or a "no" response. There is no in-between. Anything that isn't affirmative is negative. Oddly enough, a lot of salespeople are more proficient at handling a "no" than they are a "yes." A mechanism clicks in when the reply to the request for an order comes back in the negative. The salesperson goes back into a probing mode, works to understand objections, and tries to figure out any concerns or hidden objections that underlie what the customer has stated. If a provisional response can be formulated, a trial close is attempted, and the salesperson is again silent, regenerating the entire cycle.

What sometimes throws salespeople is when that initial request for an order is met with an immediate, unqualified "yes." In fact, salespeople are often trained to do exactly the wrong thing under those circumstances. There is an old, traditional school of thought suggesting that when the customer replies affirmatively, you should get out of there as quickly as you can. Get the order and run. Leave customers with that "yes" on their lips. Don't give them a chance to change their minds. The logic behind that approach is, at best, faulty. If a customer is going to have a change of mind, your absence won't prevent it. It will prevent your *knowing* about it, but that isn't exactly consistent with the concept of control.

Closing is more than simply asking for the order. A sales cycle is truly closed when you have gotten a "yes," and then secured a solid commitment from the customer that can survive a competitor's loss recovery attempt. Rather than getting away, you've got to stay close. If ever the competition is going to launch an offensive, it will be here and now, when they sense they are losing. Your presence, not your absence, is the only thing that will prevent a reversal by the customer. A good way to secure a decision is to make the decision a matter of public record. It pays to *advertise*.

Once again, put yourself in the shoes of a buyer who has just told Vendor A that he or she is going to get the order. The salesperson has thanked the buyer, said that he or she will stop by in a couple of days to pick up the executed purchase order, and then run away. At this point, only the vendor and the salesperson know about the decision, and the salesperson is in hiding. That afternoon, the buyer gives the bad news to Vendor B, who goes into a loss recovery mode, and asks for a meeting the next morning. The buyer reluctantly consents. Keep in mind that, in this situation, the order is not formally placed. Some vendor companies have policies that prohibit "unhooking" executed purchase agreements, but in this case, Vendor B's efforts to turn the situation around are on safe and ethical ground. The salesperson is going into loss recovery, not *lost* recovery.

In the meeting the next day, Vendor B makes a compelling case for the buyer to reconsider the decision. As the salesperson talks, the buyer begins to think hard, and the more he or she ponders, realizes that Vendor B is, indeed, the wiser choice. The buyer begins to ask serious and sincere questions, always a sure signal that the loss recovery effort is beginning to turn the corner.

Remember, if you were this buyer, given the evidence, what would the odds be that you'd change your mind, reverse your field, and go with Vendor B after all? What would prevent you from changing your decision? The answer to the last question is "nothing." If Vendor B's case is persuasive, nothing stands in the way of the buyer's change of heart, except for an uncomfortable, but hardly show-stopping, admission to Vendor A that he or she spoke just a bit too soon in your conversation yesterday.

Now, let's say that Vendor A operated just a bit differently in the closing process. This time, closing wasn't just asking for the order, it was securing a solid commitment. After receiving the good news that he or she would get the order, the salesperson advertised—discreetly, but unmistakably—in the organization. The salesperson made sure the vendor's staff knew what decision had been made, making sure that the Fox was advised. Rather than disappearing, the salesperson became an even more visible presence in the account, immediately working with other people to plan for implementation, to coordinate with finance, with administration, operations, and with anyone else with whom it made sense to interact.

The next day, Vendor B comes in with a loss recovery attempt. The salesperson's case is just as persuasive as before, but what are the odds this time that the buyer will be able to change his or her mind so easily? With more people aware of the decision to go with Vendor A—many of whom are enthusiastic about it—it becomes harder to alter the course. In this version of events, the green light the buyer gave to Vendor A shines more brightly than it did before. Because the salesperson stayed close and advertised, it became a spotlight on the buyer, his or her credibility within the own organization becoming a part of the equation.

By the way, I made this example simple to make a point, but I don't want advertising to seem like a manipulative tactic. In reality, you do have to work with other people in an account once you get a verbal order, and there's no reason not to start right away. It will have a salutary effect on your ability to do the best job for the customer.

Also, a customer has an interest in having his or her decision solidified. As often as a competitor will try to turn around the selection made by a decision maker, even more often they'll try to turn it around with the decision maker's boss. Securing the order and advertising the decision will prevent embarrassment for the customer as much as it will protect your position. In that respect, when it comes to selecting who and when to advertise a decision to, always center in on the Fox. He or she will then guide you further, and instruct you about other people who should be brought into the loop. It's one thing for your competition to attempt to overturn a decision maker. It's quite another for them to try taking on a Fox.

When you're in that unfortunate but necessary position of having to go into loss recovery, we've already discussed your first major objective: to get a meeting where you can discover the issues—both tangible and intangible—and begin to formulate a response. Now, a second objective becomes clear: to determine whether the competition has effectively advertised. If they haven't, at least you have a fighting chance to recover. If they have, if they've stayed close, advertised, and locked in the commitment with a Fox, recovering the loss will be considerably more challenging, and perhaps impossible. Either way, it's important to know that changing a decision is never easy for a customer. Even with an unadvertised decision, people are naturally reluctant to appear unsure of themselves. You have to provide them with the escape vehicle mentioned earlier, a way to change a decision without seeming to waffle, a way to save face. This becomes the third major step in a loss recovery effort. Some of the tactics we examined earlier can serve to provide a customer with an acceptable way to reverse a decision. For one, bringing new people onto the scene, and getting them to search for new issues, may help correct a situation that is going poorly.

When you're having problems, the customer's decision may partly be based, legitimately, on issues of which he or she is unaware. Possession of new data constitutes a perfectly acceptable rationale for changing a decision, even in a very public fashion. And, even if the new data is only, in reality, a pretext for the altered course, it still serves the purpose of helping the customer change the decision without risking humiliation.

The tactic of taking the customer off the scene, to an executive visit at the home office or to one of your key reference accounts, can also expand the customer's knowledge of you and your company in such a way that a decision's reconsideration becomes palatable. As long as factors can be introduced that represent genuine value in the evaluation process, a change can be correctly positioned in the customer's mind, and with others, as being the result of careful, thorough scrutiny before making the decision absolute and final.

In a loss recovery mode, when you successfully address issues that have caused your difficulties, you give customers reason to change the decision they have preliminarily made, or the direction in which they were leaning. To actually make the change, the ego obstacle has to be removed. That's what an escape vehicle is meant to accomplish. For it to work, you'll have to put your own ego aside. You must position everything you do in a manner that will help the customer save face, otherwise you'll never get the decision reversed. The customer didn't do a lousy job in the evaluation process—you did. The customer didn't make a mistake—you did. The customer didn't fail to consider important information—you failed to provide it. In other words, you'll take the blame. The good news is, you'll also take the order, unless you truly can't resolve your problems, and unless the competition has achieved an unbreakable lock on the business.

The weaker they are at advertising, and the more inclined they are to follow the old school and high-tail it out of the account after the first "yes," the better chance you'll have— if you're prepared.

The time to think about how to recover a losing situation is not when you first discover that you're going into a tailspin. The general's plan of battle contains a provision for retreat, which is devised well before troops take to the field. In a sales campaign, you're usually tactically active for some period of time—hopefully, a brief one—before the sales strategy can be fully developed. The quicker you reach clarity on your strategic plan, the more effective you'll be throughout the sales cycle. And the sooner you develop a provision for what you'll do if difficulties arise, you'll have a better chance of coming out in one piece.

When you're in the fortunate position of being on the winning side when an order is placed, protect yourself from a loss recovery attempt by the competition. When you get that "yes," do whatever you can to secure the commitment. Stay close. Advertise. The closer you come to winning, the closer you come to losing, even when you think you've already won. You are at your most vulnerable in the eleventh hour. Everything is on the line, and some competitors will try just about anything. Once again, however, you can anticipate desperate measures, but you will be able to deal with them in an effective and proactive manner by using a technique called trapping.

Trapping

Trapping is among the highest-order Ivy League street-fighting skills. The name sounds predatory, but the activity itself is very positive. With it, you take the high road and set standards for what a customer should expect of a vendor. At the same time, you protect yourself from unsavory moves a competitor may make. In practice, trapping is a matter of conditioning the customer environment so that a competitor's negative tactic backfires if he or she employs it. If the competitor never tries the tactic, nothing happens—the trap never springs.

Trapping an Air Strike

You've just successfully concluded a sales cycle. The customer has told you that you're getting the order, and the two of you are planning who you will talk to next. You'll be able to secure the commitment, you'll be able to advertise, and the customer definitely wants you to stay close. This is a happy moment, and you shake hands warmly with the customer. This is no time to bring up unpleasant topics, right? Well, it may be just the right time.

Suppose that you've been competing for this deal with a vendor you've gone up against several times before. In the history of those encounters, you've learned to expect your opponent to do one thing for sure when an order seems to be getting away: he or she will launch an attack from the air. The salesperson will immediately go over the decision maker's head to try to get the decision reversed. There isn't much you can do to prevent the competition from trying this, but you may be able to take steps to diminish its effect. For example, just as you are thanking the customer for the order, you may be able to set the trap. Imagine that the dialogue goes something like this:

"Harry, it's going to be a pleasure to continue working with you. I'm going to make sure this installation is a success.

You won't regret your decision. By the way, tell me, now that you've made the decision, are you ready to take the heat?"

Harry, naturally, is a bit taken aback. "What do you mean? What heat?"

"Well," you begin, "you know how some salespeople are. They find out they're not getting an order, and they go haywire. First they come in and do a number on you. If that doesn't get anywhere, they go and do a dance on your boss's desk. Of course, if they're clever, they're subtle about what they say to someone like Carl. But you know what the real message is—that you've made a bad decision, and in a very real sense, that you're incompetent. Do you think Carl would stand behind you if something like that happened?"

This may not be the best rendition of a trap being set in its purest, most subtle form, and but I think you can see the effect it's aimed at achieving. You want George to get a little hot under the collar just at the *thought* that a vendor would try something like that. You want him to feel righteously indignant, and to take steps to make sure it doesn't happen. Ideally, you want George to go into Carl's office and say that he's made a decision, and ask if *Carl* is ready to take the heat. When Carl asks what George is talking about, you want the conversation to go something like this:

"Well, boss, you know how some salespeople are. They find out they've lost an order, and they go nuts. Next thing you know, they're in here, dancing on your desk and telling you what a jerk I am. Are you ready for that? Are you going to stand behind my decision?"

Pity the vendor who tries to go over George's head when a good trap is set. The salesperson will be lucky to get an appointment with Carl. If he or she does, and then walks into Carl's office and starts the routine, sparks fly. Not only does the tactic fail, it blows up in the salesperson's face. This somewhat whimsical trap was set late in the sales cycle, but traps can be set at a much earlier stage. They'll almost always spring, however, toward the end, because that's when the competition will usually attempt desperation tactics. That is also when a trap will have maximum effect. Early in the game, having a tactic backfire is embarrassing. Late in the game, the effects are more telling. Traps do not create competitive advantage as much as they create disadvantage for the competition. Best employed, a trap is set indirectly. Inferences, rather than statements, make them most effective. Since you really have no business talking about what the competition may or may not do, you have to rely on the power of suggestion.

Trapping for Drastic Price Cuts

Some vendors out there will try to buy business. As a sales cycle nears its climax, whether they think they're doing well or poorly (usually the latter), some salespeople will get their management to approve offering the customer a dramatically lower price. On the surface, it seems that your only response is to try to match it, or to at least come close and minimize the difference. However, you do have another option. By setting a trap, you can not only cause a reaction, but also educate the customer and provide a sense of perspective about priorities. Sometimes the net effect of the process is to get the customer to ask your competitors tough questions.

Early in the sales campaign, you may want to have a frank discussion about your company's approach to pricing. Your product's prices are set as they are for a reason; there's a rationale behind it. A company must maintain margins. Without them there's no profit, and without profit, all the intangibles that go with a product tend to suffer—intangibles such as support, service, and the kind of R&D that will ensure migration paths. If a company is willing to slash prices by 40 percent at the eleventh hour of a sales campaign, as tempting as that may be to a customer, there are really only a few things that will come of it, none of which are very admirable. For one, it may mean that the customer won't receive support service to which they would normally be entitled. It may result in their having to purchase services that are customarily bundled in at no charge. What will the pricing structure be for those services? Will it be fair, at a reasonable margin? Who knows? By that time, the customer is pretty much at the vendor's mercy.

On a broader scale, that great deal may cause some other unfortunate soul to miss out on services, or to be forced to pay inordinately for them. From the customer's perspective, that may not seem so terrible, but look down the road a bit. Someday, the shoe may be on the other foot, and the customer may end up indirectly paying the freight for someone else's bargain basement prices. Even worse, the whole business of slashing prices seems a bit manipulative. After all, if the price comes down 40 percent right before the decision, perhaps it was artificially high three months ago, when the sales cycle started. What was the vendor trying to pull? Was it the old high-ball low-ball game, or would they have stayed with the old price if they thought they could get away with it?

By having this kind of discussion with a customer, you can set a trap for one of your competitiors: when he or she comes in offering the big discount, the reaction may be far different from what was expected. Again, you want the customer to ask that competitor some tough questions: "We appreciate your trying to be cost effective, but how can you offer such a dramatically lower price? What will I be giving up? What will this cost me in the future? Why didn't you offer such a good deal from the outset?" In addition, another smoldering question is being expressed non-verbally: "Is this salesperson trying to manipulate me?" For your opponent, what once seemed a sure-fire way to get the order has now become an inexorable problem. He or she probably can't give a credible explanation, and certainly can't go back to the higher price.

Notice that, in this process, you didn't say a word against the competition. You talked about your approach, and explained your philosophy to doing business. You set the standard, and in the process, the trap. The competition walked right into it, impaling themselves. You didn't disparage them, and you didn't negative sell. In fact, negative selling is very much an activity you can trap against.

Trapping Negative Selling

As we've discussed earlier, there are bound to be casual, informal, relaxed conversations with a customer during a sales campaign. It's important to use these opportunities to accomplish informal objectives, and trapping is one of them.

Off-the-cuff conversations give you a chance to learn about a customer from a personal point of view, and also to reveal something about yourself. For example, it's very natural to talk about how long the person has been with the company, where he or she has been before, and what the future may hold. Almost any conversation of this nature eventually becomes a two-way street; at some point, it's only polite for the customer to solicit a little bit of information about you.

Now, imagine that you have a competitor who's been trashing your company from one end of town to the other. In some accounts, this person has been able to heighten the focus on some of your company's problems to such an extent that it has created real difficulties for you. This time, in your casual conversation with the customer, you're going to trap that salesperson, before the trashing begins. Instead of giving a quick rundown on how long you've been with the company, where you went to school, and all that, you try to describe some of the values that are important to you. You don't simply say that you enjoy working for your company, you explain *why* you do. It may be because the company has standards and principles, and puts a premium on professionalism. There may be some things your company would never stand for, such as disparaging other vendors. For one thing, that just isn't professional. For another, it's a little questionable. Why do some people do it? Why do they spend more time ripping up their competition than they do telling their own story? Do they have something to hide? What does that mean about their attitude toward customers? Do they think customers are too uninformed to evaluate vendors on their own?

As you talk, you advise the customer about problems and challenges that your company is facing, and what you're doing to address them. You offer to provide the names of people in your other accounts as references, if the customer would like them, as a tangible demonstration of your company's commitment to its clients. You're not preaching in this conversation, you're just telling the customer something about yourself and your company, along with what he or she can expect from you in terms of professionalism. At the same time, you're laying down a minefield.

In comes your competitor. With the first disparaging comment about your company, there's a boom. The salesperson continues, and there's another boom. The salesperson is confused, but goes on. More booms. Now, the salesperson is really puzzled. Everyone else has been taken aback by the horror stories he or she has told about your company, but this

157

customer is reacting differently. This customer tells the sales-person to stop talking about the competition, and to get on with it. This customer starts to ask tough questions that imply the salesperson is hiding something. This customer is beginning to get angry. The trap has sprung.

There are a number of reasons why negative selling is a bad idea. At the top of the list, though, is the pure and simple fact that it's easy to trap for. There's no substitute for a good sales strategy, but a series of well-devised traps comes close. At times, they can create so much competitive disadvantage that you'll win almost on their strength alone, with the added benefit of keeping you always on the high road.

The Amalgamated Trap

In the previous chapter, we left the Amalgamated sales situation after having changed the ground rules so well against Comcorp that they fell out of the sky. Unfortunately, we also discovered there was a likelihood that you were left in a horse race with Quadtex. Quadtex, you'll recall, has been running a "me, too" direct strategy against Comcorp. Even with the ground rules changed, they have a chance to stay in the game by going "me, too" again. They may not know it, but you do. Quadtex can offer the same kind of advanced product as yours, so you need a way to make what you predict they will do work against them. You need a good, solid trap to put Quadtex away for good. As you recall, you came into this sales situation late, and initiated the shift in buying criteria with the submission of a proposal. Let's pick up the story at that point. We will see how you can actually capitalize on your late entry, and at the same time, set the trap for Quadtex. The dialogue might go like this:

"Before giving you this proposal, I should apologize for being a little on the late side, but I wanted to be sure that I had an accurate understanding of exactly what you were looking for. I also wanted to take the time to be sure my company's proposal was a team effort with our best people. I don't want to be the kind of salesperson who just walks in and tells you what I think you want to hear—I can imagine how you would react to that. No matter which way you decide, I want to present an approach that represents my company's very best thinking."

This sample dialogue may be a little rough around the edges, but I think you can see its intent. Coupled with a sincere regret for causing the customer inconvenience is a desire to set the bar rather high—at about Adam's apple-level—for the competition if they do what you suspect they will.

The ground rules change, and in comes Quadtex, saying, "Okay, we've got one of those, too." Now, what is the customer's reaction? Spoken aloud or not, it goes something like this: "Is 'me, too' the extent of your sales vocabulary? Why haven't you given serious thought to my needs, and applied a little creativity? Why do you only tell me what you think I want to hear? Is this what life would have been like had I bought from you?"

Mind you, some very significant things happened here. You dispatched Comcorp by turning their strength against them. You knew what Quadtex would do weeks before they knew what they would do. And when they did it, you made it blow up in their faces. You controlled the sales environment, and you managed the competition. These are the victories you can savor the most. At the start, you had little chance of winning. The Comcorp salesperson probably had already forecast the business. You took it away.

It may have been even sweeter. People in your own company may have thought you couldn't win this deal. But you did. Some call people who win the unwinnable "heroes." I call them Ivy League street fighters.

Chapter 11

The Political Strategy

Make your way by unexpected routes.
—Sun Tzu

In the Amalgamated scenario, the success of the indirect strategy is inexorably linked to your political skills. If you fail to profile that organization's Power Base of influence, never finding someone who, given the right motive, has the opportunity and means to change the ground rules, your approach will not succeed. Real competitive advantage, then, comes from following a road not usually taken in a sales campaign. It comes from combining a formal sales strategy with an informal, political one. Even when you are weak in a sales situation, an intelligent political strategy, by itself, may still produce competitive advantage. And when you are strong, it can give you competitive *immunity.*

A political strategy involves advancing the *personal agenda* of someone who can, in turn, help you win business. In this way, a synergy develops between you and a key person in the account, much as we discussed earlier in the case of John Andrews in Chapter 2. Now it's time to get into more detail about this very critical component of a competitive sales campaign.

Personal Agendas

A personal agenda represents what an individual *personally* wants to obtain as a result of the value he or she brings to the organization. With people whose agendas are weak, there is usually only one thing they want from their companies: money. They want to earn their pay and go home. There are other people, however, who are more ambitious, and it is around them that you can center a political strategy. They, too, want to be reasonably compensated, but they are also somewhat driven. They want to make a mark. They want to leave work each day having accomplished something special. Often, what they ask in return is the opportunity to advance in their organizations. This is a very common agenda for people you encounter in sales situations, people who really have some influence in the buying decision. It is also an agenda to which a skilled Ivy League street fighter can make an important contribution.

Behind every agenda is a key ingredient, some factor that is critical to whether the agenda will be fulfilled. For people wishing to advance, this ingredient is usually "visibility." These people need to have a definite, positive image in the eyes of those who will make recommendations and decisions about promotions.

It's not a good idea to make assumptions about personal agendas. You really have to learn what they are from their source. It's also a mistake to place value judgments on someone's ambitions. For example, let's say a large New York-based company has a field office in Texas, where a regional manager has been in the job since 1975. Over the years, many people who held similar positions for less time have already worked their ways to higher levels in the firm. In fact, this regional manager reports to a vice-president who used to work for him. If you had this company as an account, you might be inclined to assume that the regional manager is about as far away from being in the Power Base as he can get. Insight about his personal agenda, however, may change your mind.

As it happens, this fellow's personal agenda is to stay exactly where he is. His wife has a business of her own in Austin, so relocation for her is entirely out of the question, and what's important to her is important to him. In addition, he has always been very involved in the community. He can't give civic affairs all the time he'd like to, but he doesn't want to give them up, either. This person is no less ambitious than anyone else in the company, he's simply making his way by a different route. His personal agenda is "stability," and the key ingredient for anyone whose desires center around building and maintaining a solid base is "support."

In many respects, the regional manager's agenda is more challenging than if he simply wanted to move up in the company. The higher you get in an organization, the more you become an impediment to the progress of others if you linger in the position. Any setbacks you experience are more easily attributed by others to your having held the job too long. Besides, even if you're not moving up, someone else is—and every time the players change at senior levels, this regional manager has to realign himself politically. Like anyone, he will need to tend the home fires in terms of being recognized for the value he contributes. His value must be linked to the benefits of his staying in charge in Austin. To establish them, he will need support, and that would be the basis for your political contribution to his personal agenda.

Advancement and stability tend to be agendas focused on the long term, but some agendas are short term in nature, and equally receptive of your assistance. To explain this better, let's examine what would induce, from a political point of view, Bob Evans to work on your behalf in Amalgamated.

Power Struggles

In Chapter 9, we introduced Ellen Murphy as Amalgamated's CFO for quite a long time. She started with the company twenty years ago, on the same day as the man who is now president, and they've worked closely together ever since. Her loyalty to him, plus a great deal of hard work, has paid off over the years as she has moved up the ladder. The president has a good grasp of fiscal affairs, but relies heavily on Ellen Murphy to count the beans, which she does with relish. She has never acted in anything but the company's best interests, but does possess an extraordinary amount of control. Bob Evans, who is vice-president of operations, has no problem with her personally, but believes her approach is entirely too conservative at a time when it is essential for the company to be aggressive. Other members of the senior management team have similar concerns, but Murphy is not without strong support, which is why the process of acquiring the company's computer system is in her hands. Losing control over a project that was his idea nettled Evans, but it was only one battle in the ongoing struggle within the company to redefine its direction and culture. Other battles he had won, but this one had slipped away—until you came along.

What is generally not known within Amalgamated, because senior managers have agreed to keep it quiet for now, is that Evans has already won a significant battle. On the executive level, the decision has been made that an MIS department will be created, and that it will, sensibly, be part of Evans' operations department. Evans won the MIS war partly because of a compromise that was struck. To placate conservative members of the management team who were concerned about his aggressiveness, it was decided that Ellen Murphy would have control of the vendor selection process for the company's first major automation investment. In other words, Amalgamated has instituted an example of the kind of programmed conflict or contention management we discussed earlier.

Bob Evans' agenda centers around *competition*, a natural and healthy contention in Amalgamated at a critical period in its history for who will shape the organization's direction. Evans is doing political battle, and like any general, the key ingredient for fulfillment of his agenda is "supply lines." Since control of a company's direction is usually not obtained in one fell swoop, but is gathered gradually, piece by piece, Evans got some measure of control by winning MIS. But his victory was tempered when Ellen Murphy won control of the decision. The score is deuce, and the only question that remains is who gets the next serve.

When you, a politically astute Ivy League street fighter, came into the picture, you brought supplies—value—that put the racquet back in Bob Evans' hands. You brought the value of a good product and the good sense to link everything you did to what was of value to the company from a business point of view. When Evans acted to change the ground rules, he did so partly because of the tangible advantages he saw in you and your company, but also because he saw bigger-picture political gains to be had. When the rules changed, and you won, he gained a good measure of self-determination for the MIS department he was to create. You, then, were a catalyst for political change in Amalgamated.

Power Plays

There are limits to how fully you can safely get involved in the politics of an organization. Your participation must always be governed by the awareness that you're operating in an area where, technically, you don't belong. You'll recall from Chapter 3 that Carol Miller had a similar problem. Every time she exerted influence outside her formal domain of marketing, she had to operate quietly and behind the scenes. In this respect, you share certain restrictions with a Fox.

Only one of the four classes of strategy applies to a political strategy: indirect. Your involvement in the politics of an account can never be overt. Your political contribution to a key person can never be directly proposed. Often, you can't even make statements, but must count on inferences being drawn from the questions you ask. What gets tricky about providing political value is the formula we covered earlier: as your value increases, your risk decreases. The more political value someone like Bob Evans sees in you, the more your risk of losing the business goes down. But you can carry it too far. You can get so involved in politics that you lose perspective. You forget that your job is selling, not being High Counsellor of Bob Evans' war camp. You become intricately and overtly involved in the politics. You start to make public pronouncements in the account about how operations, not finance, should be driving this decision. And suddenly, your risk goes up exponentially. You become a slow, very large target that Ellen Murphy can shoot out of the sky with one hand tied behind her calculator. Some people will lead you down this road to destruction. In Amalgamated, there is a power struggle between Bob Evans and Ellen Murphy. Both are acting from legitimate points of view in the best interests of the company.

A "power play" is when someone does not have the good of the organization at heart, but is only working to advance his or her own selfish ends. A power player in Bob Evans' position wouldn't strive for control of MIS for the benefit of Amalgamated, he would do so only to satisfy his ego needs for dominion over a large empire. He wouldn't support your proposal because it's best, he would use your work to make life difficult for his political enemies. As much as power struggles are healthy in organizations, power plays are parasitic. Instead of nourishing the company, power players feed off of it. They are also the first people to try to get you to do things that just aren't right, that get you overly involved in politics. Someone in Evans' shoes who does not work from a basis of positive intent might induce you to say things in an open meeting that are completely out of line, perhaps simply by putting words in your mouth. He might squeeze you for information that others have shared in confidence. He might induce you to turn various people in the organization against each other.

As soon as you start feeling squeamish about something a contact in a sales situation asks you to do, turn away. Trust your instincts. Fan out in the account, drive up value with other people. Bring in colleagues to help you in the account so you can distance yourself somewhat from a power player. Always remember, these people really don't care what happens to you. When you get thrown out of the account, they still get something they wanted. Even if they've only disturbed and sidetracked their opponents for a brief period of time, they're happy.

In Amalgamated, we were lucky that none of the major players were coming from the dark side of the force. Bob Evans is a good person, and so is Ellen Murphy. But we've forgotten someone.

Remember Henry Walker?

When we first examined the Amalgamated account, the key person wasn't Bob Evans. It was Henry Walker, the supervisor of the data center. Ellen Murphy has given him the responsibility to select a vendor, but had reserved final approval for herself, and made her preference for Comcorp clear. Now let's move back in time and complicate the Amalgamated sales scenario just a bit. You may recall your first meeting with Bob Evans. It went remarkably well. His perspective definitely clicked with what you wanted to propose. He stepped in on your behalf, facilitated the change of the ground rules, and you won. It was almost too easy. So, let's put another spin on that meeting and see what happens.

As before, the formal part of the discussion goes very well. Evans is more open and enthusiastic than you could have dreamed he would be. He's given you his perspective on the business direction of the company, and you've completed an impressive presentation about your company and its product capabilities. This time, however, he does not indicate he will work on your behalf to change the ground rules. Instead, here is what he says:

"Look, I think you've got a great solution. If it were up to me, I would tell you right now that I'd like you to be the chosen vendor. I know what you want me to do. You want me to say that I'll step in with Ellen and Henry and broaden the selection criteria to give you a shot. But I'm sorry, I just can't do it.

"I'd like to be able to work with you and your company. Confidentially, I'll be forming an MIS department in the next few months, but that's not public knowledge. Anyway, there may be an opportunity for us to do business in the future. But for now, my hands are tied, the ball is completely in

Ellen's court. As for Henry, well, he's a good guy, and I think he has a lot on the ball. The big question is whether he is savvy about what this company really needs, and if he has some moxie. I guess we'll find out. Listen—I've got to run—sorry I can't help you."

The meeting wraps up, and you go on your way. What are you going to do now? I'll tell you what a lot of people would do. They would abandon their indirect efforts and revert to a direct strategy. They would immediately throw up their hands and say, "If we're going down, let's go down fighting." I guess that's gallant, if there's any gallantry in resigning yourself to losing when you still have a chance to win. There's plenty of fight left if you complete the construction of a total sales strategy.

The indirect approach we identified as being the only option represented the formal sales strategy for this account. It had a political component because we needed someone powerful to change the ground rules. We were fortunate that the strength of Bob Evans' agenda caused him to become active. But this time he's not going to do so. It's clear now that we need a separate and distinct political strategy to *augment* the formal one, to make Bob's involvement sufficiently indirect so as to be politically acceptable. In the absence of such a strategy we won't be strong contenders for the Amalgamated deal.

To create a political strategy, you simply answer three questions: who, what and how? Who has an agenda that will be advanced if the decision goes your way? What is that agenda? How can all of this happen? Of course, answering all these questions isn't quite that simple. It takes a lot of digging. You have to take every opportunity, with every contact you make in a sales campaign, to find out something about the agendas of the people you're dealing with. Then, you have to think about the key ingredient each agenda requires. After that, it becomes a process of narrowing it down to the right person. The most difficult part of the strategy is the "how?"

You have enough information about this latest twist in Amalgamated to form a separate political strategy. You may want to take a few minutes and think about how you would articulate it.

Making Your Way

The "who" can't be Amalgamated's president. We really don't know much about him. It also can't be Ellen Murphy. We don't precisely know her agenda, but the obstacles to getting her support seem insurmountable. It can't even be Bob Evans. We know his agenda—competition with Ellen Murphy—but we've already tried the "how" of getting him involved, and it didn't work. Something interesting happened during the meeting with him, though. Was your sonar working? Did you hear the pinging?

The target for a political strategy comes down to Henry Walker. You'll recall that Henry once was leaning heavily toward a high-tech solution, and liked Quadtex's newer product a lot—but he wasn't willing to go in and fight for it. Doing so would have put him at odds with his boss—rarely the best form of good corporate citizenship—at a time when he is angling for a promotion. You need a political strategy to show Henry (the "who") that his agenda (managing MIS, the "what") will only be fulfilled by understanding that his future rests with Evans, who favors your solution (the "how"). Implementing it will be a little trickier than it appears; you'll have to be very skillful.

You can imagine what some people would do. They would be unable to resist the temptation to march into Henry's office with an announcement. "Hank, I've just learned from Bob Evans that he's going to have MIS, and I got the very strong sense that if you select us, he'll name you to run it." Anything as forward as this would only lead to disaster. For one thing, there is a very strong possibility that Henry will feel just a tad manipulated. The salesperson has already done something that would make many people in Walker's position angry by effectively going over Henry's head by contacting Evans. Even if this doesn't bother Henry, because he's a mature professional, this latest presumptuousness will at the very least rub him the wrong way.

Secondly, a confidence shared by Bob Evans has been violated, and this will become a weapon in Ellen Murphy's hands. At a meeting of the executive committee, she will demand to know why Bob is telling every vendor off the street about the MIS decision, one the committee previously had agreed to keep quiet. She will also demand an explanation of why Evans is so blatantly trying to manipulate the selection process when he had previously agreed to keep out of it. Bob would be defenseless against these attacks, and he would be completely unable to respond in kind—against Ellen Murphy, that is. What he would do to you is another matter. If he's a very generous person, a kind and forgiving soul, and if he's otherwise had a very good day, about all he'll do is tear out your lungs.

Fortunately, your approach would not be nearly so blatant. You know there is only one class of political strategy—indirect—and your approach to Henry Walker would be much more sophisticated. Henry has to know what's going on, but he can't be told directly. This inherently dichotomy means that the questions you ask must be much more revealing than

171

any statements you make, particularly since there are some things you're not permitted to say at all.

Before your next meeting with him gets into what you're formally there to do, you might engage in one of those off-the-cuff conversations I've mentioned before. You might make reference to your meeting with Bob Evans, relate how valuable the insight was that you gained, and ask Henry to tell you a little more about Bob. What kind of guy is he, personally? The odds are that Henry will tell you a lot of things you already know, but there's nothing wrong with that. You'll probably also learn some things you didn't know. But what *you* learn isn't nearly as important as what *Henry* becomes aware of. In asking more and more questions about Bob Evans' role in the company, you want Walker to become highly conscious of exactly how much clout Evans has.

You'll transition at some point in the conversation into asking where Henry sees the organization going, and how it will be affected by the automation project. Henry is bound to mention that an MIS department will have to evolve; at that point some very natural questions from you would be, "Who will own it? Would it make sense for it to be part of finance, or is there a likelihood that it would come under operations?" You're not violating Evans' confidence, you're just trying to get Henry thinking.

You might conclude your dialogue by asking whether he is planning to conduct a thorough needs analysis with Evans, since it was clear to you that Bob had very specific ideas about the approach he would like to see taken. You could even add that Evans had very nice things to say about Henry. To some people, this approach sounds manipulative. That's partly because the reality of what you do in a sincere, genuine effort to make a contribution to someone's agenda is almost impossible to recreate on paper. But it's also because some people don't believe you should even be trying to make such a contribution. But let's face facts. Whether or not you become politically involved in this situation, there is going to be a political effect. Bob Evans is getting control of MIS, regardless of what happens here. If Henry makes a "savvy" decision—as Evans put it— and shows a little "moxie," he will get promoted. If he blindly stays on his present course, he will be running the finance department's data processing center for the rest of his life, unless Evans gets control of that, too. You aren't manipulating anyone or anything.

Another concern some people would have is that this approach leaves a lot to chance, or more specifically, to Henry Walker's intuitive powers. That's true. If Henry doesn't pick up on the signals, you're going to lose. There is nothing ironclad in any strategy. With this one, though, you improve your odds from zero to something much better.

Fortunately, there's a pleasant outcome in this version of the Amalgamated story, as well. It may have taken you a few tries, but all the questions you asked finally prompted Henry to ask a few of his own. The minute he called Bob Evans and asked for a meeting to discuss Bob's perspective of system requirements, Evans heard something besides Walker's voice on the phone. He heard the unmistakable echo of your political sonar pinging back, returning with a response of "message received." Then, when Henry and Bob had their meeting, and Bob's first statement was how much he liked your company's solution, Henry began to sense that there might be something going on here. Later, when he directly asked Ellen Murphy where an MIS department would report, and she refused comment, he _knew_ something was going on here. When Henry Walker submitted his complete analysis of requirements and the selection of you as vendor, he knew that Ellen Murphy still had the right to disapprove the decision, and that Ellen might not be entirely happy with his conclusions. But at the very least, he knew he had some protection, a shield that arose when you connected his agenda with Bob Evans.

For his part, Evans was not passive throughout this process. Your work with Henry allowed Bob to work behind the scenes. In the days before Henry formalized his recommendation, the word somehow spread throughout Amalgamated that the company was actually going to try something innovative for a change. Expectations began to be raised. Evans even mentioned at an executive committee meeting how impressed he was with Henry Walker's thorough approach to the automation project, and gently needled Ellen Murphy about what he had heard was coming in the way of vendor selection. "You're really getting wild, Ellen," Evans teased. "We're going to have to find a way to keep yours and Henry's aggressiveness in check." Even Amalgamated's president said, in this meeting, how good it was that the company was addressing its needs creatively: "We're going to have a few things to show this industry by the time we're through." Finally, by the time Henry Walker put the papers on her desk, the ground rules had even changed in Ellen Murphy's mind. Remember the trap you set for Quadtex? You actually set it with Ellen. That's how much things changed once your political strategy started to take hold.

I've always wondered how people in the Comcorp salesperson's place tell their management they've lost a deal that everyone thought was in the bag. I have a feeling that they first talk about how hard they fought for the business, which may be true. A lot of the time, I bet they tell management they got sandbagged and were misled by the customer. That isn't true. At the end, they probably tell their managers that they had the deal won, but then it came down to politics. That is definitely true. What they don't know is that it always does.

Part Three: Zeroing In

Chapter 12

Should I Compete? Targeting Your Opportunities

He will win who knows when to fight,
and when not to fight.

—Sun Tzu

Not every sales situation provides the opportunity to successfully compete from within and defeat the efforts of opposing vendors. There are times when nothing about the ground rules favors you, and no potential exists to change them. Conditions will arise when not even a small crack appears that allows you to enter with a divisional strategy, and when the door is closing so quickly that the competition's momentum simply will not be contained.

In an account, the importance of knowing whether you have a good chance of succeeding is only surpassed by *when* you know it. At the end of a sales cycle, everybody knows. The window of opportunity becomes a narrow aperture through which only one vendor can pass, and the factors that determine either victory or defeat become abundantly apparent. None of this is clear at the beginning of a sales campaign, except to those who gain an advantage by having an orderly way of narrowing the aperture early. Traditional methods in this regard just don't cut it.

You don't gain much insight by making an instinctive best guess as to whether the customer will "buy, buy now, and buy from me." All you get out of that kind of guessing is the inclination to chase everything that has a pulse. Evaluating whether to compete is critical, but the decision doesn't stop there. All sales opportunities are not created equal; different opportunities have different levels of sales potential, and require different levels of effort from you.

Developing vision early in a sales campaign is a function of building a "target acquisition" process. Insight comes from having an objective mechanism that allows you not only to select a target, but also to determine how vigorously it should be pursued *compared to other opportunities*.

Some sales opportunities clearly should represent *primary* targets for your efforts. Substantial and ongoing revenue potential, or strategic significance from an overall marketing perspective, should compel you to give them a significant amount of time and attention. In contrast, other targets should be judged as *secondary* in importance. Perhaps they are unlikely to close in a reasonable period of time. If so, they may be of less significance today, but can't be written off entirely if they have the potential to become primary at a later date. Still other accounts should be classified as *tertiary*. These are known in military circles as "targets of opportunity." You'll pick them off if you can do so easily, but you won't let working on them compromise your efforts in more lucrative accounts. They may represent short-term business, and although that's important, there are times when you're better off sitting in the lobby of a primary account than pursuing a tertiary opportunity.

Classifying opportunities as primary, secondary, or tertiary seems simple, but the process of doing so can become somewhat vexing when it is applied to the real world. There can be a fine line between a primary target and a secondary one. In addition, conditions will arise when accounts that appear primary should be treated as secondary when you take a hard look at all the opportunities in front of you. Most of us have a tendency to pursue everything that is active. If it's warm and breathing, we go after it, and before long, we have a focus problem.

A more objective approach involves constructing a template of specific, known criteria to overlay on an unknown situation. Generally, no single one of the criteria we're about to cover can determine the degree to which a sales opportunity has potential, or the extent to which you should pursue it. They must be used in concert with one another, in order to help you make that critical decision as to when to fight, and how hard.

Criteria 1: Location

The most logical place to begin considering the extent to which sales efforts should be devoted is the account's location. Even before examining the other criteria, a targeted account should be one where you can establish a sales presence with a reasonable investment of time in travel. This is not to say that a local account should be automatically considered a ripe primary target, or that a remote one should always be relegated to secondary or tertiary status. Both kinds require full examination, but the remote account does call for a heightened level of scrutiny. When an account is remote, you obviously must consider whether you will be able to devote the time it will take to sell into it, particularly if it is going to be a highly competitive situation. It is difficult to manage an account from an arm's-length distance. It's hard to know what's *really* going on when you telephone a customer; his or her overly polite and succinct tone of voice could mean that a competitor is sitting right there in the office.

A look into the future is also called for—if you win the deal, will your company be able to support it? If there are no resources close to the account, you would be wise to determine if you will be able to give it all the hand holding new customers tend to require. You owe this to the prospective customer, and it's in your own best interests, as well.

Criteria 2: Application Compatibility

Your initial look through the window of opportunity in a sales situation should not be focused on what you want to do, or on what the competition wants to do, but on what the customer wants to do. These are the ground rules, which may remain fixed throughout the sales campaign, or change.

Buying criteria remain fixed when they are based on real, irrevocable, and specific needs. Suppose that you are selling electronic components to a defense contracting firm. The buying criteria call for a product that has certain security features that are mandated by the Department of Defense. You've got a great product, but it, unfortunately, lacks that one feature.

Forget about changing the ground rules; there is an inherent incompatibility between your product and the customer's need or application. Drop this opportunity right into the tertiary category. You may still work on it, there may be value in merely establishing a presence for future opportunities. But you'd better not put it on a forecast.

On the other hand, suppose you're selling medical equipment. One large hospital is expanding its range of services, hoping to attract a broader base of patients. They have put out for bid a requirement for CAT-scan equipment with the first of a series of specific applications in mind. If your product is weak in addressing the first application but strong in future ones, might you be able to change the ground rules? You would certainly have a better chance in this case. Buying criteria become greatly more flexible when they are based on emotional or subjective factors. This is not to say that changing them will be easy; as we've already found, a lot depends on the political strength of those who have created them. But here, at least, your product is not definitely excluded from the range of customer options. Your job will be to get it added to their considerations.

Criteria 3: Installed Base

Being the installed vendor doesn't guarantee that you will have competitive advantage, but it does suggest a good leg up. You have been through the decision making process before, you're a known entity and, hopefully, you're politically aligned. For the competitor, all this may be new. Having this presence, assuming the installations have been reasonably successful in the eyes of the customer, should cause you to weigh the opportunity more heavily. On the other hand if it's a new account, be careful not to deprioritize it. After all, it could be a golden opportunity to drive a little competitive displacement.

Criteria 4: Financial Condition

The desire to make a significant acquisition is often doused with the cold water of financial reality. Even for projects that are planned and underway for some period of time, committed funds vanish at the eleventh hour far more often than hoped-for monies miraculously appear. A sales campaign that ends with a decision to buy being cancelled altogether is not a "no-decision," it's a loss. The time and effort you devoted—resources that could have been spent on other opportunities—can never be recovered.

For your own protection, you are obligated to perform a financial sanity check on the fiscal health of an account where a major buy is expected. You should begin at the macro level, and proceed from there to a finite, micro view, which we will address in Criteria 5.

For the big picture, you do not need to suddenly develop the skills and expertise of a CPA. Simply by reading business periodicals and newspapers, you will develop an understanding of the trends and issues in your customers' industries.

More specific sources are available that, even if you only have a general understanding of finance, help you gauge the health of a company and the industry it's in. The most easily obtained of these is a company's annual report. We all know we should read annual reports, and the whole process of obtaining one involves either a telephone call to a company's corporate location, or a trip to the local library. But you would be surprised to know how many salespeople never read even their largest customer's annual report. You would be even more surprised at how many salespeople don't read their *own* company's annual report, which makes forming a sense of company-to-company business value—and communicating it to senior people in an account—extremely difficult.

A few items in the back of any public company's annual report will give you a snapshot of the corporation's fiscal health. The Balance Sheet freezes a moment in time, and allows you to make some fundamental determinations. For example, you can measure a company's ability to meet its responsibilities and support growth by figuring the current ratio, simply by dividing current assets (cash, marketable securities, accounts receivable, and inventory) by current liabilities. A standard rule of thumb is that the ratio should be at least three-to-one, but actual good health indicators vary from industry to industry. If the ratio came out close to even, you would have to be concerned about this company, as capital for acquisitions may not be available. In such an instance, you would next want to see if the company can get cash if they need it. When the debt-to-equity ratio (long-term debt divided by shareholder's equity) exceeds, as a rule of thumb, 30 percent, a company may have an extremely difficult time finding sources for borrowing. Essentially, it's a measure of a company's ability to raise credit.

Another component of a financial report is the Income Statement. Rather than capturing a moment in time for analysis, the Income Statement tallies what in a fiscal period has come in to the company, what's gone out, and what's left. From the Income Statement, figure the company's net profit margin by dividing net pre-tax income by total revenue. Then, compare the recent historical trends of net profit margin to total revenue. If revenue has been growing but the net profit margin has not, the company may not be managing the operational costs of its growth very well. It's just another indication that trouble might be on the horizon.

Some of this may sound complicated if you don't have much experience reading financial reports. But, believe me, with just the description I've provided, you can perform these calculations in less than ten minutes. You can also pick up a good book on corporate finance and learn many more insightful calculations to perform. It's not important to become an expert in high finance. The only thing that matters is that if the opportunity is big enough, you draw at least some preliminary conclusions about what life is like financially in the company you're about to sell into. For that matter, it's not even vital that your conclusions be 100 percent correct. From your analysis, you get a basis for some very good questions to ask in the account, the answers to which may help you refine your vision of what business value you can offer. Of course you'll have to temper your findings about the financial picture with your experience in, or knowledge of, the customer's business. In some industries, buying can screech to a complete halt when money is tight. As a result, some otherwise primary opportunities would have to be considered secondary only because of the likelihood that the sales cycle will be extraordinarily protracted.

In other industries, just the reverse is true. Some automobile manufacturers, for example, are known to make most of their major capital acquisitions when business is at its worst, particularly when the acquisition is directly related to achieving economies of scale and returning to profitability. For you, what's important is to know whether you will be part of the problem or part of the solution.

Criteria 5: Funding

Real insight about the impact of finances comes when you couple the broad view with an examination at the micro level. To do this, you examine whether funds are specifically earmarked in the budget for the product you hope to sell or for purposes directly associated with it. You should take a very hard look here, and come to a binary conclusion. Funds are either designated, or they're not. There's no in-between. Now, by comparing what you learn at the micro level with the big financial picture, you can begin to look at the financial influences that could make or break your securing an order. For example, what conclusions would you draw if the financial picture of the customer is very rosy, but if no funds are budgeted for a product they intend to buy? The first thought that may come to mind is that there is actually very little chance that a purchase will take place; that the customer must place little value from a general business perspective on the acquisition. That is a very real possibility. Any doubt in your mind should be confirmed before considering the opportunity primary.

Another perspective is that this apparent contradiction means nothing. It may be that the customer simply hasn't gotten around to transferring the appropriate funds, but will when the decision draws near. In that case, it is perfectly appropriate for you to confirm with whomever has control over the funds (definitely a member of the Power Base, by the way) that the necessary capital will, in fact, be available.

Let's turn the situation around. Suppose the customer's financial condition is weak. Its Balance Sheet is a sea of red ink. They're laying people off; senior managers are taking a crash course on Chapter 11. Nevertheless, budget monies exist for acquiring a product that you are bidding on. What would you think? On the first cut, you would have to suspect that the funds are going to disappear. But then again, it may be that acquiring a product such as yours is required, and absolutely essential to putting the business back on track.

Often, as you can see, the more financial information you get only produces more questions for you. But, the answers could be instrumental in assessing the financial viability of

185

your winning the business, not to mention keeping sales cycles as short as possible.

Criteria 6: Driving Mechanism

A good way to cut through the fog as to whether an acquisition will actually take place is by discovering whether a driving mechanism exists. A driving mechanism is some impending event or circumstance that is *compelling* the customer to buy. It doesn't mean that they'll buy from you, but it means they'll definitely buy from *someone*, because they have no choice.

In our hypothetical example of the Amalgamated account, a strong driving mechanism existed. That company needed to acquire a computer system to maintain their competitive position, and had to wrap up the selection in four weeks before funding expired. Few stronger driving mechanisms could exist.

When a company is opening a new office, there is a driving mechanism for certain products. Desks and other office furniture must be acquired. Arrangements must be made for telephones, other equipment, and certain building services.

When a company takes on a government contract, it usually must agree to specific performance clauses. Deadlines and completion milestones must be met, or the contract itself will be in jeopardy. If installation of a product such as yours is essential to meeting requirements, a driving mechanism exists.

If the customer has plenty of cash, but none of it is budgeted for the purposes associated with your product, the presence (or absence) of a driving mechanism will tell all. When the customer is financially strapped but still has funds earmarked for a product like yours, a strong driving mechanism will allow you to still consider the opportunity a primary one, while a weak one would suggest that you view the prospect of an order being placed rather skeptically.

A good question to ask in any sales campaign is "Why do you want to buy?" However, to get at the driving mechanism, your question must be a bit more specific: "What will happen if you *don't* buy?" Ask *that* question early and often. Even if you already know the answer, ask it of someone you're convinced has the big picture. Anyone who can't answer it isn't in the Power Base—one more way to scope out the political structure.

With all the data we've covered so far, plus the size of the order and time frame for a decision, you can frame the potential of a sales opportunity. Some factors are more important than others, but combined, they give you the most accurate first-pass view of whether the opportunity represents a primary, secondary, or tertiary level of importance.

Criteria 7: Customer Competence

If there's anything worse than losing an order, it's winning one that, six months later, you wish you had lost. Not all sales opportunities are created equal, and neither are all customers.

Some salespeople prefer to have prospective customers who are novices. The knowledge and expertise then resides with the vendor, allowing the salesperson to, perhaps, better manage the sales situation. He or she takes on a more consultant type of role, providing advice and direction as well as a good product solution. Other salespeople prefer to work with prospects who have been around the block once or twice. The good thing about selling to these people is that they don't wear rose-colored glasses; they know what to expect, and you don't have to spend a lot of time educating them.

187

There is a good case to be made for either end of the spectrum, and there are risks associated with both. Selling to novices usually involves more time, because of the required education process, and you run the risk of educating them just well enough that they buy at a lower price from someone else. The experienced buyer will often press you harder for concessions, and sometimes block you from dealing with other people in the account.

Being objective, whether a customer is a rookie or a seasoned veteran, you still should ascertain whether he or she is competent from the standpoint of the resources you will have to pump into the account. If training or other support is going to be required, make sure it will be adequate to do the job.

On a more subjective level, one where you should also come to some conclusions, a person's ability or knowledge is not nearly as important as his or her attitude, at least in terms of deciding whether the *prospect* will become a *customer* you can live with. What often makes the difference is whether key people in the account subscribe to a concept called "transfer of ownership."

All customers have a right to expect things of you and your company after the point of sale, even beyond whatever ongoing service and support they pay for. But for some customers, a day arrives when the product or service they acquire is *theirs*. In their minds, the responsibility for making it work belongs to them. Sure, they'll need your help from time to time, but that's all you can do—help. Getting everything they should from the product is in their hands. For others, ducks will be born wearing bow ties before this happens. Three months after installation, you'll walk into the account to find out what all the problems have been and why your support people spend long days and nights there. The first thing you'll see, sitting right next to your product, will be the user manuals your company provides, pristinely encased in their original shrink-wrapping, untouched by human hands.

When you gently suggest to the customer that a good way to avoid problems in the future would be for people to learn basic troubleshooting and diagnostics, he or she will respond with a grave shake of the head and a tap on your company's logo on the product, saying, "That's not my company's name. This is *your* product. *You* make it work."

Suppose, due to time constraints, you had to choose between working on two opportunities. If all things were equal except for customer competence, you would obviously give priority to the account that presents the best profile of a long, fruitful relationship. Whether you would pursue the other account at all would entirely depend on whether you believe you could manage the difficulties you predict you'll encounter. The time to do that is not when the order is placed, but as early in the sales campaign as possible.

Criteria 8: Short-Term Potential

Some companies define the short term as thirty days, while others might view it as a six-month period, but whatever the time frame, it is a key criteria for most salespeople. What makes it so important is the reality of being on quota where some amount of business simply must be short-term. In making this assessment, however, the challenge is not in defining the right time period, but in understanding the interplay with other criteria. Funding, financial condition, and driving mechanism are what make short-term potential real. If these don't exist, be cautious. A customer may have short-term intent, but that won't get you an order when you need it.

Criteria 9: Repeat Business Potential

Closing business this month, this quarter, or this fiscal year is always going to be at the top of a salesperson's list of priorities. But generating revenue next quarter or next year can be a close second, particularly as quotas tend not to go down. For that reason, repeat business potential should always be a priority for you. Giving it emphasis makes sense from two perspectives. For your company, a pipeline of business lowers the cost of sales, which has a direct impact on the bottom line. For yourself, the same principle applies: with repeat business, you lower your own cost of sales, in terms of time. When a string of business is recurring for you almost automatically, you extend your capacity to open new accounts.

Separately, each of the criteria we've covered provide you with a level of insight that most salespeople never obtain. Together, they answer that very important question: "Should I compete, and if so, to what extent?" If, however, they don't answer this strategic question, you may want to go a step further and actually assign a weight to each criteria. Experiment with a scale that quantifies each of the nine criteria and then apply it to several known sales situations. With a little experience, you'll soon have a means to compare new opportunities with those you are already addressing. If you left it just at that, you would begin a sales campaign with far greater vision than most salespeople will have even at the end. But there is even more to consider. Having decided to do battle, the next question is: "Can I win?" In Chapter 13, we'll examine this question in terms of four criteria that will either spell victory or defeat.

Chapter 13

Can I Win?

*He who is destined to defeat first fights
and afterwards looks for victory.*

—Sun Tzu

Even in situations where it absolutely makes sense to compete, there is no guarantee that you have a strong enough position to win. Early in the sales campaign, you must look at your strength—beyond what your company's product and reputation offer—to determine what you're going to have to do to win. By doing so, the battle for business will be fought and won in your mind well before it is officially decided.

Let's construct another hypothetical sales situation. We won't even bother to name the account, competitors, or type of product involved. All we'll do is look at a set of favorable circumstances and see how easy it is for them to produce nothing in the way of an order. Here's the story. You're doing very well in your sales territory. Things are running so smoothly that you have time to add more prospects to the pipeline. You have scanned your territory and analyzed a number of opportunities. From these, you have selected one as a primary target for your efforts. The account you've chosen looks very attractive. You work in a relatively small geographic area, so location isn't an issue. You can get to prospects, and if you win, your company can support them.

As for application compatibility, your product provides all of the major features the customer is looking for, plus a few that stand out a bit. No vendor has an installed base in the account, so it's an open game.

When it comes to real need in making a purchase, this customer has it. There is a strong driving mechanism, and absolutely no question that a decision will be executed as planned within three months. Their financial condition is very strong—business has been good—and they've budgeted sufficient funds (more than adequate, actually) for a sizeable acquisition.

In brief, this opportunity is loaded with short-term potential. But wait, it gets better. The long view is equally handsome. This account has been planning to bring in the product or service like the one you sell for quite some time. Their people are trained, the resources required for success are in place. History also shows that they take both physical and emotional ownership of everything they acquire. As if this weren't enough, there is strong potential for the customer buying more of the product they acquire over the next couple of years, in increments that eventually will represent more than triple the original investment. If there ever was a dream primary account, this is it.

Now let's talk about how you could lose it.

Criteria 10: Access to Upper Management

The first mistake you can make in this hypothetical account is to enter at too low a level in the organization. Many salespeople prefer to do this because it's easy to get access to lower level people, and they're not difficult to communicate with. As the cycle progresses, salespeople rely on lower level operatives to introduce them to management, if it becomes necessary. I can't say that a bottom-up approach won't ever work, because it can in many situations. But there are real risks in operating this way, and a much higher chance of losing control.

The mistake many salespeople make when working from the bottom of an account is that they think they don't have to bother gaining access to senior management, unless something goes wrong, unless it becomes critical. They decide to cross that bridge when they come to it, and assume that shifting into a sales mode more focused on executives won't be terribly difficult. On all counts, they are wrong.

We've already discussed, much earlier in this book, the perils of being blocked by a Non-Influential Non-Authoritarian who assures you that the decision is his or hers to make, and who tells you in no uncertain terms not to talk to anyone else in the account. Keep in mind that this person, in addition to road-blocking your access to other people and points of view, is also depriving you of the opportunity to provide anything but product value to the account.

Forget business value; it is the rare lower level individual who understands anything but the bells and whistles of the product under consideration. Forget political value, because you only know one agenda—that of the lower level person's—if he or she even has one.

The longer your access to other people is blocked, the more competitively vulnerable you become. As the cycle begins to peak, and you finally decide you're in trouble, what you really have on your hands is a disaster. It's too late to try to ramp up the value you represent. Providing business and political value takes work, a lot of preparation, and time. Putting all this together in the eleventh hour is virtually impossible. In addition, if only at the end of the process you decide to damn the torpedoes and break the block, there is virtually no way to do it painlessly. The moment you decide to go over your contact's head, you also decide, consciously or not, to make this person very unhappy.

If this had happened earlier in the sales campaign, it wouldn't be nearly as much of a problem. It would represent a tactical difficulty, one from which you can usually recover. Early on, when you have someone whose feathers are ruffled, you have time to smooth them. Late in the sales campaign, this isn't a tactical problem, it's a strategic one, and strategic problems are usually fatal. There isn't time to smooth those ruffled feathers when days remain before the decision, so you're going to pay for it. In reality, you don't just have a strategic problem, you've made a strategic error. It's an error because you could have completely avoided getting into this jam.

There are a number of ways to prevent being put into this position, or more precisely, to avoid putting yourself into it. Let's start with the velvet before getting to the sandpaper. The first, and perhaps best, alternative in a situation where a lower level person tries to block you is to explain exactly why you must have access to other people. Explain how your approach is going to be based on making the best business contribution you can to the company, and that to do so you must get the broadest possible perspective. Often, lower level people recognize the value of your doing this, and will actually support you. If one of them fails to see the light, don't let your persistence ebb. Many companies establish informal policies that require salespeople to interact with senior managers in accounts. Explaining that you must adhere to such policies can help you in just this kind of situation. If your company doesn't have such a policy, you may want to suggest that one be implemented. If such reasoning with a lower-level person fails, you may have to take firmer measures. You may have to ask one of your company's executives to schedule an appointment with a senior manager in the account. This, too, will probably ruffle some feathers, but again, you can usually recover.

If all else fails, you still have the option to ignore what the customer has told you. You could go ahead and get a meeting with senior management. When your contact becomes angry, you can, again, explain your need to achieve the broadest possible perspective relative to their company and its needs. Remember, it's early, so you have time to calm the waters.

The best way to avoid getting blocked, however, is to call on someone high in the account before you talk to anyone else—someone as high in the organization as is possible, and appropriate. This isn't to say that your first contact must be with the chairman of the board, but you should err on the high side when deciding at what level to kick off your campaign. The worst thing that can happen when you call high is that you will get referred down to someone lower, and that's not a bad thing at all because you can develop influence from it.

Suppose you decide to make your first call in an account to a senior vice-president. Because you know that people at this level have a broad set of interests well above specific product issues, you do your homework. You read up on the organization, peruse its annual report, and formulate a plan for an initial telephone contact to establish credibility from a business point of view, with hopes of scheduling a meeting. You place the call and, somewhat to your surprise (but undoubtedly because you sound like a business person, not just another salesperson), the secretary puts you through to the executive. You have a short conversation, where you describe your intent to work on the project that is being undertaken in the company, and your hope to contribute in some way to helping the organization meet its objectives. You say that before you start rattling around in the company, you want to take your direction from the vice-president, based on his or her perception of critical business needs. Unless asked, you don't even mention your product. This is purely a business call; it is not telemarketing.

This has been a very brief conversation, and it ends when you ask the executive if there is a convenient time for the two of you to meet in the near future. If your approach is strong, there is a very good chance this senior vice-president will agree to meet with you. You'll gain a lot in that meeting. You'll learn what's really driving the decision from a general business perspective, and you'll get incredibly valuable insight to the company's Power Base.

Of course, your approach could be very strong and still not get you an agreement to meet. The executive simply may not have the time and you may get referred down, but as I said, there's nothing wrong with that. All you have to do is thank the senior manager, assure him or her that you will immediately contact the recommended individual, and politely ask permission to report back on your progress in the next couple of weeks. I can almost guarantee you that your request will be granted.

With this process, whether you get the meeting or not, you cannot be blocked by a lower level person. It simply can't happen, because when you contact that individual, you'll say that you've been referred by the senior vice-president, and you've promised to report back with results in the next couple of weeks. Quite frankly, that lower level individual still may get angry, so you might have some peacemaking to do. But because it happened early, you have time to do it, and you're dealing from a position of strength. I don't want to sound harsh, but in a very real sense, the angrier that person gets, the better you should feel. Such a reaction should convince you that you did the right thing, that this person would have put you in a box, given just a sliver of a chance. All of this should emphasize how critical it is for you to work credibly at higher levels in organizations. In fact, quite a bit of the process we've covered in this book can't have very much effect if you lack that ability.

If working with senior people is new to you, there's only one way to learn, and that's by doing it. It can be stressful, but there is absolutely no substitute for developing real power on your own, to being able to compete from within. You can practice in your own organization. Schedule a meeting with one of your key executives to discuss where the business is going, what critical issues it faces, and how it represents value to customers in a unique way. You'll not only get good information, you'll get a feeling of what life is like on the top floor.

In our hypothetical account, making the first assessment of your chances of winning is whether you have access to senior management. If you have it, you're moving in the right direction. If you don't have it, you must work to get it as soon as possible. The longer you don't have a presence at the top, the more opportunity you give the competition to establish theirs.

Criteria 11: Understanding the Decision-Making Process

The second major criteria to consider in assessing your win-potential is whether you truly understand the *real* decision-making process that exists in the sales campaign. In many respects, your ability to do this is directly related to the level of people you're dealing with in the account.

Every decision has a formal set of criteria that will ostensibly determine its outcome. Sometimes the elements are put down on paper in a "decision matrix." In the version I've illustrated in Figure 13.1, what various vendors (listed vertically) offer is rated according to a set of buying criteria, which are listed horizontally. I've intentionally kept this as simple as possible, with only a few basic factors.

As you can see, Vendor A is strong in the aspects of price and delivery. Vendor B rates well in delivery and support. Vendor C looks good on price and support. Which vendor will win? To get the answer, you simply decide who you *want* to win. If you prefer Vendor A, you place more emphasis on price and delivery than you do on support. To give the order to Vendor B, you simply make delivery and support more important than price. To make Vendor C's day, you allow price and support to take precedence over delivery. The decision, then, is not going to be based on a clinical consideration of objective criteria; it's just been made to appear that way. The real decision-making process is set as someone subjectively assigns weights to the various components. You could easily focus on the "objective" buying criteria and ignore what lies

	Price	Delivery	Support
Vendor A	Good	Good	
Vendor B		Good	Good
Vendor C	Good		Good

Figure 13.1. Decision Matrix.

198

behind them. In that case, you could be doing all the right things with all the wrong issues, blowing away the competition on some points when the battle is, in reality, being fought elsewhere.

Understanding the *real* decision-making process requires that you know more than just the stated specifications a product to be acquired must possess. Someone in our hypothetical account has established the criteria, and has the power to set the weighting. That person (or those people) also has the influence to add new criteria or adjust the weighting at any time. Until you know who those people are, the political structure of the account, and until you know what *motivates* them to favor one vendor, criterion, or feature over another, you don't understand the real decision-making process. You are instantly vulnerable to a competitor who does.

Criteria 12: Compatibility of Philosophy

The factors of access to upper management and understanding of the true decision-making process are, for the most part, within your control. An element more difficult to influence is when there is a fundamental incompatibility between the account's business philosophy and your company's values.

We addressed compatibility in the previous chapter in terms of whether proposing your product, based on its capabilities, makes sense as a way to meet the customer's needs. Now we'll take a broader view and address the question of whether it makes sense for your two companies to do business together. Suppose you sell for a company that seeks advantage in your industry by offering added value products. The major needs of your customers can be met by a number of vendors, but what makes you stand apart is a product that technologically goes the extra mile, plus a firm commitment to ongoing service and support. Naturally, your product is a bit more expensive than others, but many customers value your advantages, so you and your company are doing very well.

Not all customers, however, are alike. Some have different priorities. Let's say that in the dream account we've been examining, their business philosophy has a sharp edge to it. You learn that from senior management on down, when it comes to dealing with vendors the philosophy of the company is that all products do the same thing. In addition, you find that the customer is very price-driven, so the lowest bidding vendor always wins. People in this company view such things as service and support as intangibles, which don't amount to much in their book.

Given what your company offers, and what it relies on for position in the industry, there may be an inherent incompatibility of philosophy between you and them. As good as the sales opportunity may look, the win potential may be so low that you should consider passing entirely on devoting any real effort to obtaining an order. To win, you would either have to effect a fundamental shift in the customer's values or in those of your own company. That is a very tall order. The good news is that occasions will arise when a strong compatibility of philosophy will exist for you and a prospective customer, one so compelling to both sides that you gain a significant advantage over the competition. What becomes important in situations like this is to be sure to capitalize on your common set of values.

Mark McCormack gives a good example of this in *What They Don't Teach You at Harvard Business School* (New York: Bantam, 1984). McCormack relates how Pepsi struggled for years to get into Burger King, a Coca-Cola stronghold. With a view toward Burger King's "have it your way" philosophy,

Pepsi implemented a sales approach that highlighted the benefits of offering fast-food customers a *choice* of soft drinks. Pepsi was perfectly willing to peacefully coexist with Coca-Cola in Burger King, but the company's management wasn't buying. Pepsi didn't understand that "choice" was incompatible with Burger King's philosophy. The company's business strategy was to ensure a quality menu by strictly limiting it; having two soft drink suppliers just didn't fit in at all. The real compatibility between Pepsi and Burger King was that they were both "number twos" in their industries. When Pepsi realized this, and began to base their sales approach on their natural affinity with Burger King, they won more than the business they had been coveting so long. Rather than having to live side-by-side with Coca-Cola, Pepsi displaced them in the account.

The prospect of not competing for business because of disparate philosophies can be a bitter pill for many salespeople to swallow, so think of it this way: you won't find a single CEO of a corporation of any decent size who wants 100 percent of the market. There is always a segment of the population that you would simply prefer not to do business with, or that you essentially cannot work with, because your perspectives on value are so different. Rather than fighting for the business, and afterward looking for a victory that just won't come, the wiser course sometimes is to find another battle. Other opportunities are out there, ones where it makes much more sense to compete, because you have a better chance of winning.

Criteria 13: Political Alignment

The final element to consider in deciding whether you can win the business you'd like to compete for regards the level of political alignment you've achieved. The political value you represent, your "hook" into the agendas of people who see personal benefit in working with you, is the single most important criterion we've discussed.

The most obvious sign of a lack of political alignment is when you lose business. But just because you win doesn't mean you've aligned politically. It may simply be that the customer has done a better job of buying than you have of selling. Without political alignment, a Fox will be the architect of your strategy in a sales situation. You will just be along for the ride. Even if you have an installed base in the account, you won't be in the driver's seat. When you don't provide political alignment, other people tend to use you for their own purposes. They'll make you a political yo-yo, and they know how to do some neat tricks.

At some point, you must achieve political alignment. You're just too vulnerable without it. If you don't align yourself politically, you can be sure someone else will, either directly or indirectly. Even if a competing vendor doesn't purposely create intangible value, if the customer perceives political advantages in going with one vendor over another, a political link is formed, and you are much farther behind in the campaign than you know.

As quickly as you can, find people who have a history of providing value above and beyond the call of duty, or who have the potential to do so by working with you. Connect with people who are on the fast track in their companies, or who have a chance to get on it when you help them succeed. Focus on learning everything you can from these people about their business, so you can define a larger contribution. Develop the kind of relationship that encourages them to introduce you to other valuable people, instead of blocking your access.

Get to know their agendas, figure out a way to assist them, and make sure they know you can do so.

In a situation where it clearly makes sense to compete, determine what factors will go into winning before the battle is most fiercely fought. To win anything worth having, you must first win it in your mind.

Political Alignment Evaluator

Political alignment is not an all-or-nothing condition. There are various levels to which you achieve it. To help you assess yours in an account, I've included the following brief evaluation instrument. It can be used early in a sales campaign and throughout the cycle to measure your progress. By answering the questions, you can determine whether someone you are working with is a "contact," a "supporter," or a true "ally." There are significant differences between the three.

Contacts are people from whom you get information, but that's about all. They're neutral, at least to you. They don't assist you in the sales effort, either because they can't or won't. If they are lower-level people outside of the Power Base, they *can't* help you win. They just don't have the power it takes to do so. When senior people—especially influential members of the Power Base—rate as contacts, it usually means that they *won't* help you. It may be that they are politically aligned with a competitor. It may just mean that you haven't given them a personal incentive—a connection with their agendas—to align with you. The condition isn't permanent, but you'll have to work to change it.

Supporters are people who, as the name implies, support you in your efforts. While you tend to work *for* contacts, you work *with* supporters. Their assistance can be significant, but they may not have the ability to help you create demand, and their support tends to relate only to the short-term nature of a current project.

To create demand, and to build for the future, you need an ally, someone with whom you share values about the short-term and *the bigger picture. These are people you do business with.* An ally not only assists you, but also is someone who is willing and able to act on your behalf, even in your absence.

Using the evaluator, after you total up the ratings and determine where you stand with a key person, you can look back at the questions where you scored low. This will give you insight about what you have to do to align politically with that individual.

Select one person you believe is important in his or her organization, and in the sales campaign you're waging. Then answer the following questions on a scale of 1 to 5:

- 1 = Untrue
- 2 = Mostly untrue
- 3 = Sometimes true; sometimes untrue
- 4 = Mostly true
- 5 = True

1. My discussions with this person have touched upon potential opportunities beyond the current known situation. ____
2. This person has a reputation for providing value above and beyond the call of duty. ____
3. This individual seems to have a clear vision of his or her future in the company. ____
4. This person has introduced me to influential people in the account. ____

5. This person seems to have a clear strategy, or wants to develop one, for establishing my company as the preferred vendor.   ——

6. In general discussions, this person and I talk about our business relationship extending in time, beyond the current sales opportunity.   ——

7. This person has been very open with me in discussing his or her company's plans, projects, and personnel.   ——

8. If asked, this person could describe *my* personal agenda, and how this sales opportunity contributes to its advancement.   ——

9. This person, from time to time, has taken the initiative in leading the sales cycle, or has assisted me in doing so.   ——

10. My business relationship with this individual transcends the current sales situation.   ——

                                           Total   ——

$$10–29 = \text{Contact}$$
$$30–39 = \text{Supporter}$$
$$40–50 = \text{Ally}$$

Drawing Conclusions

Just as with criteria one through nine, ten through thirteen can be assigned a scale not only to evaluate your "can I win" position in a number of accounts, but also to look at any given opportunity from the viewpoint of your competition. Let's assume that your "should I compete" score is high and that the same is true for your major competitor. On the "can I win" side, however, suppose that you assess yourself as being low and the competition as high. It doesn't take much to see how an assessment now could become reality later. The key is to then factor the ten through thirteen results into your sales plan where specific tactics are dedicated to driving up the "can I win" score. What you're doing is proactive in nature. You're assessing your competitive position, identifying weaknesses, and then, with targeted focus, working to improve your position. Given a green light on the one through nine, some salespeople will actually take each of the ten through thirteen criteria and re-express them as objectives to be accomplished during the sales campaign. This forces the need to put a plan in place for each criteria-objective. But perhaps even more important is that such an approach is the signature not of a salesperson, but of a competitive salesperson, the latter representing a very new breed of strategic and streetwise individual.

Epilogue

Anatomy of a Sales Force

Most people have two favorite topics, themselves and what they do, and although this is not necessarily bad, it has created a problem. American companies, over a period of time, have become inwardly focused. It is no surprise that when high technology companies experienced a flattening in the marketplace during the mid-1980s they began to renew their commitment to customers. Responding to a need to bring customers into the foreground IBM coined the phrase "year of the customer," and other companies followed suit with similar efforts to make their sales organizations more sensitive to the customer and their needs. It became clear that vendors cannot supply high quality solutions if they don't really understand a customer's particular problem set.

But something else happened in the mid-1980s that most high-tech companies were not prepared for—the number of competitors increased. The fight for a smaller piece of the market-pie became fierce. IBM moved large numbers of people out into field positions to increase coverage. Other companies actually consolidated the focus of their sales organization onto large, major accounts to selectively increase coverage. For the first time, companies could only grow marketshare by directly taking it from competition. While the inward focus problem desensitized salespeople to the customer, it had a devastating effect in their ability to deal with competition. It was a true blind spot.

Salespeople simply didn't have a competitive orientation. Their view of selling was to work hard, understand customer needs, configure good solutions, and then work diligently to project the value of those solutions to customers. And, if the customer saw that value, they got the business. This was good thinking in the 1970s and 1980s, and was an approach that fueled the growth of many a company, but in the late 1980s and into the 1990s, life has and will continue to change. The competitive environment has become extremely intense as avoiding lay-offs and holding, much less growing, marketshare becomes critical. Vendor-offered solutions need to be more than good, they need to be positioned relative to the competition's efforts to secure the same business. They need to be positioned relative to the entire customer environment, not just needs. You can have a great solution, but if you're at the wrong end of a power struggle within the customer's organization, you get blown away. Not only do you lose the business, but it's often unclear *why* you've lost.

What we are looking at is the informal structure within the customer environment, where influence is not necessarily synonymous with authority; where lower level people may wield considerable clout without it being at all obvious. After all, influence is not visible. Only the exertion of influence is visible. When a manager uses his or her power to make something happen, particularly if it's in exception to policy or a bit out of the ordinary, that power is noticeable. For just a brief moment in time, influence has been illuminated.

Sensitivity to customer politics, in terms of the "dos" and "don'ts" that enable salespeople to professionally capitalize on the political forces within an account is an ability not easily acquired. Most people are not politically insightful to begin with, but when you superimpose a lack of true customer focus, the political subtleties and infrastructure go completely unnoticed. Not everyone in the field today, however, is suffering with this inward focus. There *is* a class of salespeople who, quite the opposite, are thriving. They are the vanguard of the 1990s. We've referred to them as Ivy League Street Fighters: salespeople who don't need the best product to win. They don't need to be selling for a company that is a household name within the industry. The economy can be up or down, they make their numbers. This Epilogue is about these people, and how to recognize and develop them.

Ivy League Street Fighters do something very well that most salespeople don't do at all. They manage, in balance, customer and competitive issues as shown in Figure E-1. All

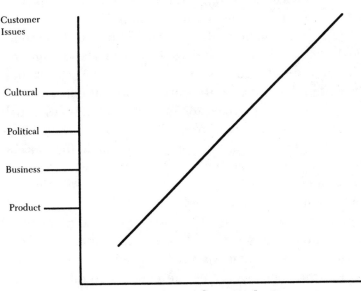

Figure E-1. Balancing customer and competitive issues.

salespeople address the product issues in a given sales situation. Beyond that, some feel that if they can understand and manage the business side to an acquisition, they have reached the epitome of customer management. In some sense they have. Many salespeople don't have a business orientation. Issues surrounding business value, cost of ownership, or competition for funds between one project and another are not easy to grasp. Additionally, salespeople who are not adept in working at the higher management levels of an account never really see the business side to what drives a sales situation. But, for those who do, a new door to customer management opens that provides an opportunity to go one step further and tap the political forces within an account. Forces that are often far more powerful than anything that could be exerted from the outside come within reach. If the salesperson is really good, he or she goes even further, bringing the two companies together in a vendor-customer partnership. Now operating at very high management levels, a cultural fit between the companies is established and managed. Business opportunities may bring the organizations together, but if the two are not congruent philosophically, the partnership will not last.

The ability to manage customer issues well is an essential quality of the Ivy League Street Fighter, but it is one that cannot exist in a vacuum. The competitive side to the process is critical. There is one and only one basic purpose to managing any customer issue: to gain competitive advantage. It is this advantage that wins orders and locks up the lion's share of business within an account. When a salesperson does a demo, why does he or she do it? To establish the capability of the product or to verify that what is being sold can actually be provided, thus enhancing the salesperson's credibility? No, these are certainly outcomes, but they are not why you do a demo. The one clear purpose is to gain advantage over the competition to advance to, or secure the order. Every tactic must have a competitive component. When a sales strategy is put in place, it must be put through a competitive counter-analysis process to determine how the competition will most probably respond. In that way, they can often be anticipated, and proactively neutralized.

As another example, competitively oriented salespeople, when asked, can tell you what they will do in the event they begin to lose. At that gut-sinking point in any sales situation, when you sense you're in trouble, when the customer is not returning your calls and you know you're in trouble, Ivy League Street Fighters switch on a preplanned loss recovery approach. They may not succeed, and indeed may be wrong in their approach, but they are not confused. This is in contrast to most salespeople who don't think about losing, much less seek out strategies to avoid it. They may have the will to win, but not the will to prepare to win.

How well salespeople manage customer and competitive issues is shown in Figure E-2, which depicts four stages of selling proficiency. It enables sales managers to characterize the strength and quality of their sales organizations, while also identifying what salespeople must do differently to become Ivy League Street Fighters.

The Four Stages of Sales Proficiency

As we discuss what life is like at each stage, put yourself or your sales organization on the scale. Be objective, assessing yourself on the basis of what you do, as evidenced by your actions in the field, versus what you would like to do in the future. We'll look at each stage in terms of four behaviors. The first is *intent*. A Stage I individual is considered an Emerging

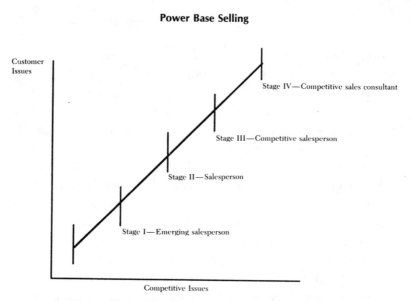

Customer Issues

Stage IV—Competitive sales consultant

Stage III—Competitive salesperson

Stage II—Salesperson

Stage I—Emerging salesperson

Competitive Issues

Figure E-2. The four stages of sales proficiency.

Salesperson, where his or her intent is simply to be considered. If Emerging Salespeople get down to a short list, they are ecstatic. Do you remember when you were at this stage? You just wanted to know that you could survive and grow into the job.

At Stage II, the Salesperson wants to make a sale. In fact, in some accounts there can even be regular "client-bashing" periods, say at the end of a quarter or fiscal year where the pressure to close orders becomes intense. For these people, each sales situation is the main event. What they don't know, however, is that making a sale is not making an account.

Elevating to Stage III, the Competitive Salesperson not only wants to make the sale, he or she wants to "own" the department. The emphasis is on repeat sales, producing a string of business. At Stage IV, Competitive Sales Consultants carry the thinking even further. They want to "own" the account, lock, stock, and barrel. They want the lion's share of the business, and to get it may structure a centralized buying influence, either formally or in the *de facto* sense. This is a person who not only services demand, but who can create it.

Figure E-3 shows the progression we have just worked through. At what level would you put yourself, or your sales organization? Take a moment and mark an X where, on average, you or your people are.

Now, let's move to the second behavior—*focus*. Emerging Salespeople center their focus on the product. They have been trained on product strengths and weaknesses and tend to view the world in that context. Moving up a stage, the Salesperson has learned that effective selling requires a view through the eyes of the customer. He or she now looks at the product from the customer's perspective, bringing closer the real needs that drive the sales situation.

At Stage III, the Competitive Salesperson certainly doesn't lose sight of the product and customer, but, in terms of what it will take to win, focuses on the competition. They represent the counter-force to success. The Competitive Salesperson takes ownership for what the competition does in his or her accounts.

Behavior	I Emerging Salesperson	II Salesperson	III Competitive Salesperson	IV Competitive Sales Consultant
Intent	To be considered	To make a sale	To "own" a department	To "own" an account
(Level)	┼┼┼┼┼┼┼┼	┼┼┼┼┼┼┼┼	┼┼┼┼┼┼┼┼	┼┼┼┼┼┼┼┼

Figure E-3.

213

Competitive Sales Consultants go even further. They look beyond the product, customer, and competition to center in on the customer's customer and competition. They reconcile how their company will, over time, make a contribution to the customer's business success, thus projecting significant added value.

As with the first behavior, go to Figure E-4 and mark where either you or your sales organization resides on the Four Stages scale.

The third behavior brings us to *relationship*. At Stage I, the word relationship is a misnomer. Remember, the Emerging Salesperson's focus is on the product, so at best, his or her relationship with the customer is a casual one.

Advancing to the Salesperson at Stage II you find the existence of a growing trust. They are able to put themselves in the shoes of the customer and project sincere concern that all goes well. In fact, it's not uncommon for a customer to even say that while a salesperson might be a little strange, you can take what he or she says to the bank. Personality is important, but quite frankly, it's secondary to knowing that you can be trusted.

Behavior	I Emerging Salesperson	II Salesperson	III Competitive Salesperson	IV Competitive Sales Consultant
Focus	Product	Customer	Competition	Customer's customer and competition
(Level)	┼┼┼┼┼┼┼┼┼	┼┼┼┼┼┼┼┼┼	┼┼┼┼┼┼┼┼┼	┼┼┼┼┼┼┼┼┼

Figure E-4.

Stage III marks the beginning of a real relationship, one that can weather a storm if something goes wrong or if the competition turns up the heat. It can be described as mutualistic. The Competitive Salesperson builds a bridge between vendor and customer, based upon value to both—not just business and product value, but political value, where the agendas of key individuals are advanced in balance with the value provided each company. You've heard of the rhinoceros and tick bird. They have a mutualistic relationship. The tick bird gets a free lunch, if you believe in such a thing, and the rhino frees himself of those pesky bugs. Sometimes, the birds will even hop down onto the mud to catch a fleeing tick and if fate has it, get stepped on by the unaware rhino. But, no problem, another bird simply flies in. That is the vulnerability of even a Competitive Salesperson—he or she can be replaced.

The fate of a Competitive Sales Consultant is less tenuous. At Stage IV the relationship is symbiotic—the two companies need each other because they are dependent on each other. It would be difficult and costly to disengage, thus bridging the companies together at the highest possible level. As before, turn your attention to Figure E-5 and rank yourself or your people.

Behavior	I Emerging Salesperson	II Salesperson	III Competitive Salesperson	IV Competitive Sales Consultant
Relationship	Casual	A growing trust	Mutualistic	Symbiotic
(Level)	┽┼┼┼┼┼┼┼┼	┼┼┼┼┼┼┼┼┼	┼┼┼┼┼┼┼┼┼	┼┼┼┼┼┼┼┼

Figure E-5.

The fourth and last behavior centers on *value*. From a customer's viewpoint, an Emerging Salesperson provides product options. The customer may even become educated by one Emerging Salesperson, simply to buy from another. As a result, life in this lane can be a scary one. At Stage II, the Salesperson has adopted a solutions approach to selling. He or she works hard to understand what the customer is trying to accomplish and puts solutions in place that provide value at the applications level. From the perspective of Competitive Salespeople, applications value is clearly very important, but they also know that if they don't couple that value with a clear expression of business contribution, they will never "own" a department, much less an account.

Moving to Stage IV, the Competitive Sales Consultant aspires to provide value at all levels, but specifically, wants to be acknowledged as having made a contribution to the advancement of the customer's strategic direction. It's a contribution at this level that allows vendors to be assertive in their pricing, to have access to long-range information which, in turn, impacts forecast quality, and, most of all, to develop competitive immunity. Completing the process, where would you place yourself or your sales organization on the scale? Refer to Figure E-6 and, if you like, carry forward the rankings for the other three behaviors to construct a total picture.

On average, where do you find yourself on the four-stage scale? My experience with salespeople within the United States' high technology companies has been that most fall into Stage II, which puts them quite behind where they need to be in today's competitive marketplace. However, these salespeople aren't there because they want to be, but because of other factors that inherently retard the growth of many salespeople.

Behavior	I Emerging Salesperson	II Salesperson	III Competitive Salesperson	IV Competitive Sales Consultant
Intent	To be considered	To make a sale	To "own" a department	To "own" an account
(Level)				
Focus	Product	Customer	Competition	Customer's customer and competition
(Level)				
Relationship	Casual	A growing trust	Mutualistic	Symbiotic
(Level)				
Value	Product options	Application solutions	Business contribution	Advance strategic direction
(Level)				

Figure E-6.

The Glass Ceiling

After years of assessing salespeople, it has become clear to me that a certain phenomenon exists: the glass ceiling. As salespeople develop and work their way up through the four stages of sales proficiency, they may notice that progress gets particularly tough at a certain point, just between Stages II and III. It is here that most salespeople tend to cluster. In

217

fact, some do very well in progressing from Stages I to II, only to crash face-first into the glass ceiling. They bunch up into a frustrated mass of humanity, able to see through, but not able to *break* through. Many, misdiagnosing the problem, blame their company and leave for greener pastures, driving up turnover.

The glass ceiling effect, in general, is not a new concept, but its application to the development of salespeople is new, and to some, a bit startling. The difficulty lies in what it takes to be successful in Stages I and II in comparison to Stages III and IV. Being a Competitive Salesperson requires not only the development of a new set of skills, but of an entirely new selling orientation. "Breaking glass" means thinking differently; it means thinking geometrically, where you are able to look at a competitive sales situation from all angles. At Stage II, success is achieved by doing an excellent job of traditional selling, but to break glass you need to look at a sales situation from the competition's point of view, putting yourself in their shoes. You need to look from the inside out, carefully examining the customer's political infrastructure, identifying power struggles and setting your alignment with the right people. Working the business issues at high levels provides yet another angle or point of view that is critical to Stage III selling.

All of these factors create a new orientation for most salespeople. Superimpose the difficulty in establishing this new type of geometric thinking on top of the need to develop a new set of Stage III skills and you have a real challenge. It is this challenge that this book aims to address. In fact, if there is one purpose of *Power Base Selling*, it is to break glass. But recognize that no book—or training seminar for that matter—will do the job of breaking glass alone. To be successful, that is, to develop a Stage III orientation and then operationalize it, requires a team effort between salespeople and their sales management.

You might think that the role of field sales management in helping you break glass is to provide support and direction. To some extent you would be right, but mostly you would be wrong. You see, this glass ceiling was originally installed by sales management. The shift in orientation and the new skills required at Stage III produce a challenge, but one that is workable, as salespeople are known for learning on the job. They adapt and learn out of practical necessity. The significance of the glass ceiling is that it puts a cap on practical, intuitive learning. Beginning in the 1970s and early 1980s, Stage II selling proved to be very successful for many companies, but it also created Stage II people. When they hit the glass ceiling, some salespeople changed companies; many others, however, moved into management. These are the people who were generally very good at being Stage II salespeople, and who are now Stage II sales managers. Lacking a Stage III orientation and, in many cases, the skills necessary to effectively coach salespeople in Stage III sales techniques, places the glass ceiling just above the heads of the salespeople. When they begin to teach themselves, either through the school of hard knocks or through books such as this one, and actually begin to make progress, they run into a very undesirable response on the part of their immediate sales management. First, their sales managers do not recognize the need for geometric thinking and, therefore, have no or little appreciation for its importance. After all, it was never needed when *they* were selling. As a salesperson, this means that your manager will not give you the support and encouragement you need to develop the necessary skills. Second, your manager may not have the ability to assist you even if he or she wanted to. The tendency is to center in on Stage II skills, and while this is certainly helpful, it misses the mark in terms of what's critical. Notably, there are exceptional salespeople and sales managers who are able to deal with all of this, but fundamentally, the world is made up of average people. The high performers in sales will succeed with or around their managers, but for everyone else the manager's role is critical, either making or breaking their success and sometimes their careers. If you're a sales manager, evaluate your people on the four-stage scale, then evaluate yourself. Where they are weak and you are strong, coach them. Where they are weak and you are also weak, train them *and* yourself by participating in programs like Power Base Selling. Breaking glass begins with you and to a large extent the impact of this book on your salespeople will depend on you—you can make the difference.